MW00901984

SAP HANA 2.0
Certified Technology Associate

By

Simon C

<u>Copyright Notice</u>

Table of Contents

Database Administration Tools and Tasks

1. Which of the following status indicator on the SAP DBCC helps us to understand whether the system meets its service level agreements or not?
   (Only one answer is correct)

   (a) Availability
   (b) Performance
   (c) Capacity
   (d) Alerts

Answer: c

Explanation:

Database control centre can be used to check the overall health of systems located within a data centre or across your enterprise. Status displays focus on four high-level areas, as follows:

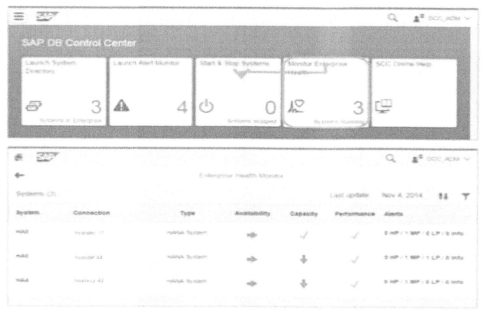

- **Availability** It is the system running and accessible on the network? Is it able to serve the business needs of its users, including humans and applications?
- **Performance** is the system meeting the response time expectations of database users, including humans and applications?
- **Capacity** is the system meeting its service level agreements?
- **Alerts** are there errors to resolve, or event messages that to review? Alert events, given priorities of high, medium, or low, are triggered when the system exceeds state and range thresholds set by system and database administrators.

2. In which of the following the situations, SAP HANA restart might be necessary?
   (There are two correct answers to the question)

(a) Database Update
(b) Hardware or Software failure
(c) Database Installation
(d) During the creation of Database User

Answer: a, b

Explanation:

SAP HANA database restart might be required in the following situations

- During planned maintenance when the SAP HANA database is updated or to activate configuration parameter changes that can only be activated by a restart of the system.
- During unplanned maintenance, due to a hardware or software failure. The SAP HANA database is unresponsive or down.

3. **In which of the following section, you can deactivate the reload feature to avoid performance overhead in the system?**
    (Only one answer is correct)

    (a) Backup section
    (b) sql section
    (c) Logging section
    (d) Memory manager section

Answer: b

Explanation:

You can deactivate the reload feature in the index server ini file by setting the reload table's parameter in the sql section to false.
In addition, you can configure the number of tables whose attributes are loaded in parallel using the tables_preloaded_in_parallel parameter in the parallel section of indexserver.ini
This parameter also determines the number of tables that are preloaded in parallel.

4. **Which of the following tool supports the starting and stopping of individual tenants?**
    (Only one answer is correct)

    (a) SAP HANA Cockpit
    (b) SAP HANA studio
    (c) SAP Solution Manager
    (d) Any third party tool integrates with SAP HANA Database

Answer: a

Explanation:

Starting and Stopping Individual Tenants

Any SAP HANA database systems running version SAP HANA 2.0 SPS 01 or later is set in multiple-container mode so it is more likely that only an individual tenant needs to be stopped or started. SAP HANA cockpit supports stopping and starting of tenant databases.

5. **In which of the following situations you have to restart an individual database service? (There are two correct answers to the question)**

   (a) When services remain inactive in a distributed host
   (b) After HANA XSA engine update
   (c) After HANA database upgrade
   (d) During revision upgrade of an SAP HANA database

Answer: a, b

Explanation:

An individual database service requires a restart in the following situations:

- A host in a distributed system failed and a standby host took over but the services of the failed host remain inactive even after the host is available again. In this case you need to restart the services manually.
- After an update of SAP HANA extended application services, you need to restart the xsengine service.

6. **Which of the following parameter controls how often the internal buffers are flushed to the disk?**

(Only one answer is correct)

(a) Global_allocation_limit
(b) Savepoint_interval_s
(c) Enable_auto_log_backup
(d) Log_mode

Answer: b

Explanation:

The savepoint_interval_s parameter controls how often the internal buffers are flushed to the disk and when a restart record is written.

After a power failure or crash the log since the last save point needs to be replayed. Thus, this parameter indirectly controls the restart time. If you set the save point to a lower value the start up shortens, but the CPU load increases slightly. If you set the save point to a higher value, the start up time increases but the CPU load decreases a little.

7. **Which of the following are the initial tasks that must be performed after the SAP HANA Database installation?**
   (There are two correct answers to the question)

   (a) Full data backup
   (b) Check the diagnosis files
   (c) Activate Additional traces
   (d) Install a valid license in SAP HANA Database

Answer: a, d

Explanation:

Performing an Initial Backup
To safeguard the changes that were made to the database it is suggested to perform a full data and file system backup after the initial setup of the system.
Installing a Valid License for the SAP HANA Database
At least one license key is required to use the SAP HANA system. This license key must be installed in the system database.
License Keys for Tenant Databases
You can install permanent license keys in individual tenant databases. The license key installed in a tenant database is valid for that database only and takes precedence over the license key installed in the system database.

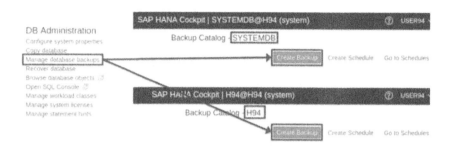

After the initial setup and the initial data load perform a
- Full data backup from SystemDB and Tenant database
- File system backup (including a configuration backup)

8. **Which of the following partitioning allows applications to be partitioned into different temperatures?**
   (Only one answer is correct)

   (a) Hash Partitioning
   (b) Range Partitioning
   (c) Round Robin Partitioning
   (d) Time selection Partitioning

Answer: d

Explanation:

Applications can use aging to separate hot (current) data from cold (old) data by using time selection partitioning to:

- Create partitions and re-partition
- Add partitions
- Allocate rows to partitions
- Set the scope of Data Manipulation Language (DML) and Data Query Language (DQL) statements

9. **Which of the following objects SAP HANA Content comprises of?**
   (Only one answer is correct)

   (a) Schemas and Table definitions
   (b) Procedures
   (c) Privileges
   (d) All of the above

Answer: d

Explanation:

SAP HANA Content
These objects are regarded as transportable content.

SAP HANA content defined:

- Not part of the core SAP HANA database installation itself
- Is delivered by SAP as part of SAP HANA optimized solutions
- Is created in SAP HANA-based development projects (partner, customer)
- Sometimes called "objects" or "artifacts"

Content comprise all kinds of objects, for example:
- Schemas and table definitions
- Attribute views, analytic views, and calculation views
- Procedures and privileges
- SQL Script, JavaScript and HTML
- Roles and permissions

10. **Which of the following system privilege is required to view the diagnosis files and delete the trace files?**
    (Only one answer is correct)

    (a) INFILE ADMIN
    (b) SYSTEM ADMIN
    (c) USER ADMIN
    (d) TRACE ADMIN

Answer: d

Explanation:

Working with Diagnosis Files in SAP Web IDE for SAP HANA:

Traces Diagnosis files include log and trace files, as well as a mixture of other diagnosis, error, and information files. If there are problems with the SAP HANA database, you can check these diagnosis files for errors. You can also filter, delete, and download diagnosis files.

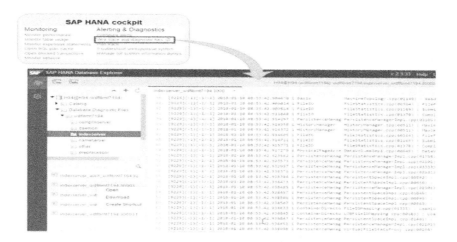

You can also view the trace and diagnostic files from the operating system level. By default, the trace and diagnostic files are stored in the following location:
/usr/sap/<SID>/HDB<instance>/<host>/trace.

Note: To view the diagnostic files and delete the trace files, you must have the TRACE ADMIN system privilege

Users and Authorization

11. Which of the following are required to model access control?
    (Only one answer is correct)

    (a) User
    (b) Role
    (c) Authorization Object
    (d) Privileges

Answer: d

Explanation:

The relevant entities relate to each other in the following way:

- A known user can log on to the database. A user can be the owner of database objects.
- A role is a collection of privileges and can be granted to either a user or another role (nesting).
- A privilege is used to impose restrictions on operations carried out on certain objects.

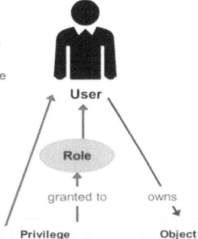

Privileges can be assigned to users directly or indirectly using roles. Privileges are required to model access control. Roles can be used to structure the access control scheme and to model reusable business roles.

12. Which of the following user type can be used for creating objects and granting privileges for a particular application?
    (Only one answer is correct)

    (a) Database Users
    (b) Technical Database users
    (c) System Users
    (d) Communication Users

Answer: b

Explanation:

User Types

Below user types can be differentiated in SAP HANA Database

Database users that correspond to real people
The database administrator creates a database user for every person who works in the SAP HANA database. The database objects that are owned by the users are also automatically dropped, and privileges that they granted are automatically revoked.

Technical database users
Technical database users can be used for administrative tasks such as creating objects and granting privileges for a particular application. Some technical users are available as standard, for example, the users SYS and _SYS_REPO. Other technical database users are application-specific.

13. **Which of the following allow you to manage related users together?**
    (Only one answer is correct)

    (a) Users
    (b) User Groups
    (c) Roles
    (d) Privileges

Answer: b

Explanation:

User Groups

Related users can be managed by using user groups. Dedicated group administrators can be assigned to manage individual user groups.

In the example scenario shown in the figure below, the user groups were created for administration purpose for each user group. Only the group admins for the restricted user group Sales can create or delete users in this user group. The Sales group admins can only manage users of the Sales group, but not users from other user groups like Research or Training.

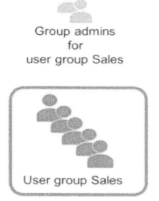

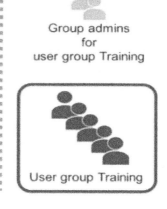

14. Which of the following users will be created automatically during installation?
    (Only one answer is correct)

    (a) <sid>adm
    (b) sapadm
    (c) SYSTEM
    (d) All of the above

Answer: d

Explanation:

The following users are automatically created during the installation: <sid>adm, sapadm, and SYSTEM.

<Sid>adm: The operating system administrator

The user <Sid>adm is the operating system user required for administrative tasks such as starting and stopping the system.

sapadm: The SAP host agent administrator.

If there is no SAP host agent available on the installation host, it is created during the installation along with the user sapadm.
If the SAP host agent is already available on the installation host, it is not modified by the installer.

SYSTEM: The database super user.

Initially, the SYSTEM user has all system permissions. Additional permissions can be granted and revoked again, however the initial permissions can never be revoked.

15. Which of the following are the reasons for having security concept in SAP HANA?
    (Only one answer is correct)

    (a) Access to ERP tables must be restricted
    (b) Database administrators to be restricted to skilled persons
    (c) Editing of HANA models should be restricted
    (d) All of the above

Answer: d

Explanation:

Security concept in SAP HANA Is required for the following simple reasons

* Database administration should be restricted to skilled (and empowered) persons

- Access to ERP tables must be restricted.
- Editing of SAP HANA data models should only be possible for "owners" of the model.

Security is important in SAP HANA as user administration plays a significant role as follows

- Several front-end tools offer direct access into SAP HANA.
- Access to object and to data model content must be controlled within SAP HANA
- Information consumers need named users in SAP HANA

16. **Which of the following are the different administration tools available for creating a user in SAP HANA Database?**
    (There are three correct answers to the question)

    (a) SAP HANA Cockpit & Studio
    (b) Command line Interface
    (c) Mass User creation
    (d) SAP Net weaver Identity Management

Answer: a, b, d

Explanation:

User Administration Tools

User management is configured using the SAP HANA studio. There is no replication of existing authorizations from source system. Below are the administration tools available for the user creation in SAP HANA as shown in the below figure

SAP HANA cockpit and SAP HANA studio
- Creating users
- Deleting, deactivating, and reactivating users
- Creating roles
- Assigning roles and privileges to users

User & Role Management
Manage users
Assign role to users
Assign privileges to users
Manage roles

Command line interface (hdbsql or other SQL Tool)
- Performing all administration tasks using SQL commands
- For example, run the following statement:
```
CREATE USER <user_name> PASSWORD
<password>
CREATE ROLE <role_name>;
```

SAP NetWeaver Identity Management
- Creating and deleting user accounts
- Assigning roles
- Setting passwords of users

17. **Which of the following privileges control the activities like creating schema, changing users and roles?**
   (Only one answer is correct)

   (a) Analytical Privileges
   (b) Object Privileges
   (c) System Privileges
   (d) All of the above

Answer: c

Explanation:

Six types of system privilege are available on SAP HANA Database:

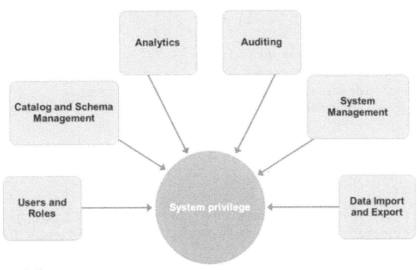

System Privilege

 System privileges control general system activities. System privileges are mainly used to authorize users to perform administrative actions, including the following:
   •   Creating and deleting schemas
   •   Managing users and roles
   •   Performing data backups
   •   Monitoring and tracing
   •   Managing licenses

18. **Which of the following privileges roles contain?**
   (Only one answer is correct)

   (a) System Privileges
   (b) Object privileges
   (c) Package privileges
   (d) All of the above

Answer: d

Explanation:

A role can contain any number of the following privileges:

- System privileges for administrative tasks (for example, AUDIT ADMIN, BACKUP ADMIN, CATALOG READ)
- Object privileges on database objects (for example, SELECT, INSERT, UPDATE)
- Analytic privileges on SAP HANA information models
- Package privileges on repository packages (for example, REPO.READ,
- REPO.EDIT_NATIVE_OBJECTS, REPO.ACTIVATE_NATIVE_OBJECTS)
- Application privileges for enabling access to SAP HANA XS applications

19. **Which of the following pre requisites are required for creating the Design time roles? (There are two correct answers to the question)**

   (a) Analytical privileges is required for the packages
   (b) Package privileges is required for the packages
   (c) A shared project must exist with a suitable package for storing roles
   (d) Object privileges is required for the packages

Answer: b, c

Explanation:

Design-Time Roles: Design-time roles are created in the development system. A developer or role designer creates the role in the repository of the development system and tests it. Therefore the following prerequisites have to be fulfilled:

- Authorization assigned: sap.hana.xs.ide.roles::Editor Developer role
- A shared project must exist with a suitable package for storing roles
- Package privileges on the required packages

20. **Which of the following are the pre requisites for displaying the privileges granted to a user? (There are two correct answers to the question)**

   (a) DATA ADMIN System privilege is required
   (b) Role name assigned to the user is required
   (c) Only a technical user is required to display the roles
   (d) User needs to be specified always

Answer: a, d

Explanation:

System tables and monitoring views query information about the system using SQL commands. System view EFFECTIVE_ROLES shows the roles of a currently logged in user. It shows both the roles which are assigned directly and from the roles which are inherited.

Display which privileges a specific user has been granted:
- Either directly or indirectly (via a role)
- Use the system view EFFECTIVE_PRIVILEGES

Prerequisites:
- When querying this system view, you always need to specify a user.
- All users can query their own data.
- For querying data about other users, they need either the system privilege CATALOG READ or DATA ADMIN.

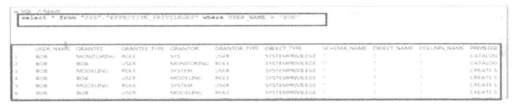

21. **Which of the following are the different authorization issues occurs for column views and procedures?**
    (Only one answer is correct)

    (a) NOT AUTHORIZED
    (b) INVALIDATED VIEW
    (c) INVALIDATED PROCEDURE
    (d) All of the above

Answer: d

Explanation:

The authorization dependency viewer helps us in identifying the invalid authorization dependencies for the objects which are large and having complex dependency structures.

Below are the authorization issues usually occur for column views and procedures. Use the authorization dependency viewer to troubleshoot the below errors.

- NOT AUTHORISED (258)
- INVALIDATED VIEW (391)
- INVALIDATED PROCEDURE (430)

Security

22. **Which of the following are the features of classic 3 tier architecture?**
    (There are three correct answers to the question)

    (a) End users have direct access to database
    (b) Database layer security is focused on administrative access to the database
    (c) End users have no direct access to the database
    (d) SAP HANA security features are mainly needed to control access of administrators to the database

Answer: b, c, d

Explanation:

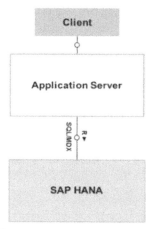

SAP HANA in a Classic Three-Tier Architecture:
- Security-related features are located an enforced primarily in the application server layer.
- The database is used as a data store only.
- End users do not have direct access to database.
- The same security model for user access applies as with other databases.
- Security in the database layer is mainly focused on securing administrative access to the database.
- User and role management is only required for administrators.
- SAP HANA Database is not accessible from the client network directly.

The classic 3-tier architecture has the following features:

- End users do not have direct access to either the database itself or the database server on which it is running.
- Security in the database layer is mainly focused on securing administrative access to the database.
- Specific SAP HANA security features are mainly needed to control access of administrators to the database.

23. **In which of the following scenario end users have direct access to the database?**
    (Only one answer is correct)

    (a) Data Mart Scenario
    (b) Classic 3-tier Architecture
    (c) SAP HANA as a Platform
    (d) Data Agile Scenario

Answer: a

Explanation:

Data Mart Scenario:

In this scenario data is replicated from a source system into the SAP HANA Database. Once the replication is completed reporting is carried out on the data in SAP HANA. Below are the features of a Data Mart scenario as shown below.

Data Mart Scenario:
- Data is replicated from a source system.
- Reporting is then carried out on the data in SAP HANA.
- User and role management in SAP HANA is required for technical users and administrators.
- End users have direct access to SAP HANA.
- User and role management in SAP HANA is also required for the end users that access SAP HANA directly.
- Direct access from client tools to the SAP HANA Database. Encryption of communication between client and SAP HANA is recommended.

24. Which of the following can be secured using TLS protocol?
    (There are two correct answers to the question)

    (a) Communication between SAP HANA database and clients
    (b) Internal communication between individual components of SAP HANA system
    (c) Communication between HANA database and Fiori Application
    (d) Communication between two systems using Storage replication

Answer: a, b

Explanation:

Transport Layer security (TLS) protocol can secure the following

- Communication between the SAP HANA database and clients that access the SQL interface of the database.
- Internal network communication between the individual components of an SAP HANA system on a single host and also between multiple hosts if the system is distributed.
- For Client Application Access, the SAP Web Dispatcher can be configured to use HTTPS (TLS) for incoming requests from UI front ends and applications, for example, SAP HANA applications. The requests are then forwarded to SAP HANA.

- Communication between the SAP HANA Software Update Manager and SAP HANA Studio, SAP Service Marketplace, and SAP Host Agent.

25. Which of the following are the features of keys and certificates used by the system PKI? (There are three correct answers to the question)

(a) Certificates are renewed automatically
(b) SAPCRYPTOLIB is used as cryptographic library
(c) Common CryptoLib is used as cryptographic library
(d) Certificates are signed by a dedicated trusted CA

Answer: a, c, d

Explanation:

PKI System Keys and Certificate features

The features of the keys and certificates used by the system PKI include the following:

- Each component receives a public/private key pair and a public-key certificate is required for mutual authentication.
- The certificates are signed by a dedicated trusted certificate authority (CA).
- The certificates are renewed automatically.
- Common CryptoLib is used as the cryptographic library.
- Depending on the communication channel, you may need to enable TLS explicitly.

26. Which of the following cryptographic libraries are supported by SAP HANA? (There are two correct answers to the question)

(a) SAPCRYTOLIB
(b) Commoncryptolib
(c) Open SSL
(d) CryptoLib

Answer: b, c

Explanation:

SAP HANA supports the following cryptographic libraries:

Common CryptoLib (default)
Common CryptoLib (libsapcrypto.so) is installed by default as part of SAP HANA server installation at $DIR_EXECUTABLE.

OpenSSL
The OpenSSL library is installed by default as part of the operating system installation.

SAP Common CryptoLib is the successor of SAPCRYPTOLIB and is the default cryptographic library for SAP HANA. Common CryptoLib is installed as part of SAP HANA server installation at the default location for library lookup: /usr/sap/<SID>/SYS/exe/hdb/libsapcrypto.so.

27. Which of the following feature is not encrypted by the persistence encryption feature?
   (Only one answer is correct)

   (a) Database Backup
   (b) Log backup
   (c) Data volume
   (d) Database traces

Answer: d

Explanation:

Data volume encryption
 Page level encryption of data volumes on disk.
Redo log encryption
 Log entries are encrypted before they are written to log volumes on disk.
Data and Log backup encryption
  Full data backups, delta data backups, and log backups.

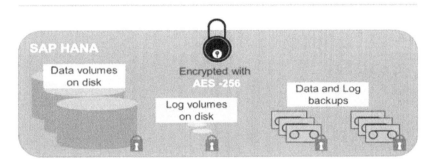

SAP HANA encrypts data volumes and redo log entries. To have a full protection in the persistence layer you can enable both.

The persistence encryption feature does not encrypt the database traces. Extended system tracing is not recommended as this feature will expose some security relevant data in the persistence layer. Enable the trace only for short term analysis for a specific task and remove the trace files from the disk once the full analysis is completed.

28. Which of the following is a column view defined on the output of a SQL script function?
   (Only one answer is correct)

   (a) Attribute views
   (b) Analytic views
   (c) Calculation views
   (d) None of the above

Answer: c

Explanation:

Attribute Views
These views are built on joins of existing column tables and views. Attribute Views cannot be nested in other Attribute Views.

Analytic Views
These views are multidimensional cubes with a fact table joined with multiple dimension tables. The information modeler allows Analytic Views to be associated with Attribute Views to reuse the specified join paths. However, it is not possible to use existing Attribute or Analytic views as base views (join candidates) and use these as the basis for defining new Analytic views.

Calculation Views
These views are defined using SQL script. A Calculation view is a column view defined on the output of an SQL script function. In this function, any existing views, including Attribute, Analytic, and Calculation Views, can be used, for example, in a SELECT statement. This introduces interdependencies between the views.

29. **Which of the following critical system events are recorded by Audit logging?**
    (Only one answer is correct)

    (a) User changes
    (b) Failed logons
    (c) Execution of procedures
    (d) All of the above

Answer: d

Explanation:

The auditing feature of the SAP HANA database allows you to monitor and record selected actions performed in your system.

Audit logging records the following critical system events

- **User management:** for example, user changes, role granting
- **System access and configuration:** for example failed logons and parameter changes
- **Data access:** for example, read and write access to tables and views, execution of procedures
- **"Log all":** firefighter logging, for example, for support cases

30. **Which of the following are the mandatory audit actions?**
    (Only one answer is correct)

    (a) Creation of audit policies

(b) Deletion of audit entries from audit trail
(c) Changes to audit configuration
(d) All of the above

Answer: d

Explanation:

If auditing is active, certain actions are always audited and are therefore not available for inclusion in user-defined audit policies. In the audit trail, these actions are labeled with the internal audit policy MandatoryAuditPolicy.

Mandatory audit actions include the following:
*   Creation, modification, or deletion of audit policies
*   Deletion of audit entries from the audit trail

31. **Which of the following are the prerequisites for configuring audit logging?**
    (There are two correct answers to the question)

    (a) AUDIT ADMIN system privilege
    (b) INFILE ADMIN system privilege
    (c) AUDIT OPERATOR system privilege
    (d) INFILE OPERATOR system privilege

Answer: a, b

Explanation:

Prerequisite: AUDIT ADMIN and INIFILE ADMIN system privilege

*   Permission to create, alter, activate, deactivate and drop any audit definition
*   Auditing can be enabled and disabled for the entire system

Switch on auditing:
Alter system alter configuration (global.ini, 'SYSTEM') set ('auditingconfiguration','global_auditing_state') = 'true' with reconfigure;

Audit policies
*   Can be enabled or disabled
*   Are stored in the database catalog

32. **Which of the following audit trial targets are supported for production system?**
    (Only one answer is correct)

    (a) Linux syslog
    (b) Database table
    (c) _SYS_AUDIT

(d) All of the above

Answer: d

Explanation:

When an audit policy is triggered, that is, when an action in the policy occurs under the conditions defined in the policy, an audit entry is created in one or more audit trails.

The following audit trail targets are supported for production systems:

Linux syslog
The logging system of the Linux operating system (syslog) is a secure storage location for the audit trail because not even the database administrator can access or change it. There are also numerous storage possibilities for the syslog, including storing it on other systems. In addition, the syslog is the default log daemon in UNIX systems.

Database table
Using an SAP HANA database table as the target for the audit trail makes it possible to query and analyze auditing information quickly. It also provides a secure and tamperproof storage location.

Audit entries are only accessible through the public system view AUDIT_LOG from an internal column store table in the _SYS_AUDIT schema. Only SELECT operations can be performed on this view by users with system privilege AUDIT ADMIN or AUDIT OPERATOR

33. **Which of the following additional privileges are there for SYSTEM user for managing tenant databases?**
    (Only one answer is correct)

    (a) Creating database
    (b) Dropping Database
    (c) Performing data backups
    (d) All of the above

Answer: d

Explanation:

SYSTEM is the database super user. It has irrevocable system privileges, such as the ability to create other database users, access system tables, and so on.

In a system with multitenant database containers, the SYSTEM user of the system database has additional privileges for managing tenant databases, for example, creating and dropping databases, changing configuration (*.ini) files of databases, and performing database-specific data backups.

In a system with multitenant database containers, **every database** container **has its own isolated set of database users**.

Whats about **System User** ?

The most powerful database user, SYSTEM is not intended for use in production systems. Use it to create lesser privileged users for particular purposes and then <u>deactivate it</u>.

34. **Which of the following is a collection of all DDL and DML privileges that the grantor currently has and is allowed to grant and can be granted on this particular object? (Only one answer is correct)**

    (a) CREATE ANY
    (b) ALL PRIVILEGES
    (c) DROP AND ALTER
    (d) EXECUTE

Answer: b

Explanation:

Object Privileges These privileges are bound to an object, for example, to a database table, and enable object-specific control activities, such as SELECT, UPDATE, or DELETE to be performed.

CREATE ANY
This privilege allows the creation of all kinds of objects, in particular tables, views, sequences, synonyms, SQL script functions or database procedures in a schema. This privilege can only be granted on a schema.

ALL PRIVILEGES
This is a collection of all DDL and data manipulation language (DML) privileges that on the one hand, the grantor currently has and is allowed to grant and on the other hand, can be granted on this particular object. This collection is dynamically evaluated for the given grantor and object. ALL PRIVILEGES is not applicable to a schema, but only a table, view, or table type.

DROP and ALTER
These are DDL privileges and authorize the DROP and ALTER SQL commands. While the DROP privilege is valid for all kinds of objects, the ALTER privilege is not valid for sequences and synonyms as their definitions cannot be changed after creation.

35. **Which of the following should be considered before changing the SSFS master keys? (There are three correct answers to the question)**

(a) System downtime
(b) File accessibility in distributed HANA system
(c) Changing of master keys for tenant database
(d) Changing of master keys for System database only

Answer: a, b, d

Explanation:

Change of SSFS Master keys

During the installation or upgrade of SAP HANA system, default master keys of SSFS will be changed and if you have received the system from a pre installed hardware vendor, change the keys immediately to ensure that the keys are not know to outside the organization

SSFS master keys can be changed using the command line tool RSECSSFX. This tool comes by default with the installation of SAP HANA and it is available at the location /usr/sap/<SID>/HDB<instance>/exe.

Before you change the SSFS master keys, note the following:

- Changing of SSFS master keys requires system downtime.
- In case of multi host system, every host must be able to access the file location of the instance SSFS master key.
- In case of Multitenant database containers, change the SSFS master keys once for the whole system and not per tenant database.

36. **Which of the following objects can be audited?**
    (There are three correct answers to the question)

    (a) Tables
    (b) Views
    (c) Procedures
    (d) Joins

Answer: a, b, c

Explanation:

In audit policy, you can specify any number of actions to audit. Only the actions which are compatible can be grouped together. Once you selected the action, any action which is not compatible with the selected action is unavailable for the selection.

In addition to the actions to be audited, we can specify other parameters as below in the audit policy.

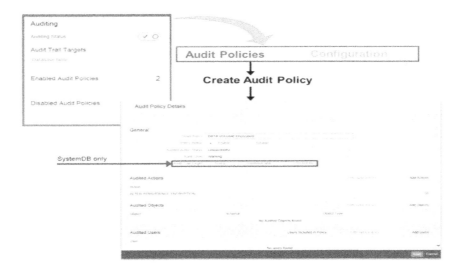

Audited Action status
- On Successful execution
- On Unsuccessful execution
- On both successful and unsuccessful execution

Target object or objects
- Tables
- Views
- Procedures

Audited Users or users
- Individual users can be included or excluded from an audit policy

Audit level
- EMERGENCY
- ALERT
- CRITICAL
- WARNING
- INFO

37. **Which of the following system privilege is required to delete the old entries from the Audit trial table?**
    (Only one answer is correct)

    (a) INFILE ADMIN
    (b) AUDIT OPERATOR
    (c) AUDIT TRAIL
    (d) SYSTEM ADMIN

Answer: b

Explanation:

Using SAP HANA Database table, you can query and analyze the auditing information. Audit entries can be accessed through the public system view AUDIT_LOG. This view is read only; only a user with system privilege AUDIT OPERATOR can delete old entries from underlying internal table.

Viewing the audit trail from the database table:

· In the SQL Console of the SAP HANA Cockpit open the view *PUBLIC.AUDIT_LOG*

· Alternatively, display the system view using SQL command:
SELECT * FROM "PUBLIC"."AUDIT_LOG"

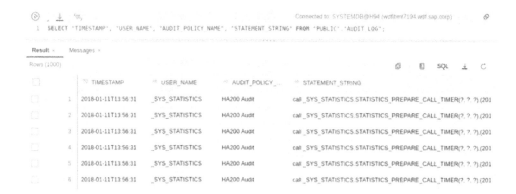

System Architecture

38. Which of the following is used to derive the static data for HANA memory requirements?
(Only one answer is correct)

(a) From the database footprint of the corresponding tables of the destination database system
(b) From the database footprint of all rows of the source database system
(c) From the database footprint of the corresponding tables of the source database system
(d) None of the above

Answer: c

Explanation:

Memory requirements for static data are derived from the database footprint of the corresponding tables of the source database system.

Database footprint in source system must be determined using database specific catalog information
- Average compression factor database table size: HANA memory = 7: 1

Note that this compression factor refers to uncompressed database tables, and space for database indexes is to be executed.
- RAM Static = Source data footprint/7

39. Which of the following options are true regarding Agile Data Marts?
(There are three correct answers to the question)

(a) Based on analytic data models
(b) No transformation during load step
(c) Data is not in original shape need transformation before loading to HANA
(d) More flexible compared to EDW Environment

Answer: a, c, d

Explanation:

- Agile Data Marts are based on analytic data models.
- Data is not in its original shape, but has been transformed before loading into HANA the level of detail in data marts typically depends on the business problem at hand.
- Agile data marts typically contain no time critical data and therefore utilize traditional ETL Direct extractor connection for SAP Business Suite extractors.

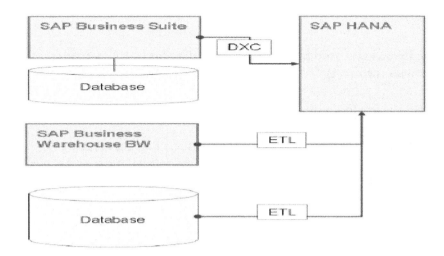

40. **Which of the following consequences will occur when you migrate the existing landscape to SAP HANA?**
   (There are two correct answers to the question)

   (a) Available application servers needs to be changed
   (b) Sizing of current app servers is invalid
   (c) Database migration to HANA is required
   (d) Co-deployment of app servers

Answer: c, d

Explanation:

Below are the consequences that will occur when you plan to migrate the existing landscape to SAP HANA

   • Migration of database to SAP HANA Required
   • SAP HANA only runs on SUSE Linux (SLES) and Red Hat Linux (RHEL)

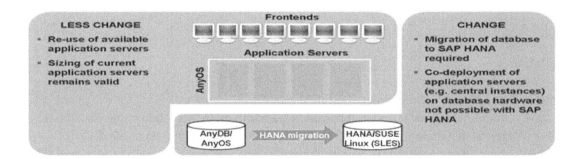

41. **Which of the following Data services function manages all your metadata and governance?**
   (Only one answer is correct)

   (a) Data lineage

(b) Information steward
(c) Metadata management
(d) Data management

Answer: b

Explanation:

Information steward manages all your metadata and data governance. The data lineage function enabled by Data Services is directly into the BI workspace of the BI end-user. By right-clicking on a number, users can choose to trace the origin of that figure back to where it comes from, how it was computed, combined, enriched etc.

This level of transparency boost trust in your BI initiative and helps users make confident decisions since they have full certainty of why a given figure is correct and what it really implies. There is also Information steward that manages all your metadata and data governance.

42. **Which of the following module ensure mapping between HANA DB and DB structure of source system in Trigger based approach?**
(Only one answer is correct)

   (a) Write module
   (b) Read module
   (c) Controller module
   (d) Migration module

Answer: c

Explanation:

DB Trigger and Table-Based Delta Logging:
  • Only relevant tables considered for DB recording
  • All relevant changes are recorded in logging tables
  • Replicated changes are deleted from logging tables
  • Recording and replication possible for all table classes
Read Module:
  • Collects data changes
  • De clustering of table classes into transparent format
Write Module:
  • Writes data through DB connection to SAP HANA system
  • Offers flexibility to switch from single operation to array operations

43. **Which of the following option allows you to select tables that are already in replication mode?**
(Only one answer is correct)

   (a) Load and Replication

(b) Stop Replication
(c) Suspend
(d) Record and Suspend

Answer: b

Explanation:

The table selection popup will look similar as for Load and Replication. In case of Stop Replication or Suspend, only those tables can be selected which are already in replication mode.
Please be aware that in case a replication is stopped and started again, the corresponding table will be dropped. The initial load must be repeated as delta recording was deactivated for a certain time and changes must be recorded.

So in case if you want to pause the delta replication, use the mode Suspend and Resume as delta recording is not deactivated and the replication can be continued without a need of a new initial data load.

44. **Which of the following is generated in SAP HANA which directly corresponds to the structure of the Data Source you are working with?**
    (Only one answer is correct)

    (a) In-Memory Data Store Object
    (b) Embedded BW System
    (c) Data load monitor
    (d) Process Chains

Answer: a

Explanation:

An In-Memory Data Store Object is generated in SAP HANA, which directly corresponds to the structure of the Data Source you are working with. This In Memory DSO consists of several tables and an activation mechanism. The active data table of the In Memory DSO can be utilized as a basis for building data models in SAP HANA.

45. **Which of the following statements are true regarding sizing in SAP HANA?**
    (There are three correct answers to the question)

    (a) Sizing of SAP HANA is mainly based on the required memory size
    (b) Sizing recommendations apply for certified hardware only
    (c) It consist of Disk sizing and CPU sizing
    (d) Sizing of SAP HANA is mainly based on required CPU and Disk sizing

Answer: a, b, c

Explanation:

Sizing of the SAP HANA appliance respectively database server is mainly based on the required main memory size. Memory sizing is determined by the amount of data that is to be stored in memory.

In general the sizing of other components within the server is derived from the main memory size. In accordance with the appliance model certified pre-configured hardware solutions are offered that comply with the sizing regulations.

SAP HANA sizing consists of

- Main memory sizing for static data
- Main memory sizing for objects created during runtime (data load and query execution)
- Disk sizing
- CPU sizing

46. **Which of the following statements are true regarding disk sizing?**
    (There are three correct answers to the question)

    (a) Disk size for persistence layer is equal to SAP HANA server's main memory
    (b) Minimum size for the log volume is equal to the size of the SAP HANA server's main memory
    (c) Minimum size for data volume is equal to the size of the main memory
    (d) Total data volume size must be at least 3-4 times the size of the RAM

Answer: a, b, d

Explanation:

Disk Sizing:

- Disk size for persistence layer:

> **Disk persistence = 1 * RAM**

Additional space must be reserved for executables and exports.
This space does not cover requirement for backup.

- Disk size for log files /operational disk space:

> **Disk log = 1 * RAM**

Disk sizing distinguishes between the persistence respectively data area and the log area. While the persistence area stores data that is kept in memory persistently, in the operational disk space log files are stored to ensure that changes are durable and the database can be restored to the last committed state after a restart.

- The minimum size for the log volume is equal to the size of the SAP HANA server's main memory.
- The minimum size for the data volume is equal to the size of the main memory plus additional space for exports and executable.

SAP recommends reserving approximately another 2-3 times the RAM value for these purposes. Hence in total data volume size must be at least 3-4 times the size of the RAM. This is due to the fact that the data volume must be able to hold:

- Space for at least one process image in case of software failure (1x)
- Space for one data export (1x)
- Shared volume (across 1multiple nodes) for Executable, other data visible for all nodes (up to 1x)

47. **Which of the following factors are influenced in more complex query scenario additional CPU requirements?**
(There are two correct answers to the question)

(a) Data Volume
(b) Query Complexity
(c) I/O resource
(d) User activities

Answer: a, b

Explanation:

CPU Sizing in Complex Scenarios In more complex query scenarios additional CPU requirements are influenced by the following factors:
Data volume: The resource requirements for queries increase linearly with the amount of records that have to be processed.
Query complexity: Queries with computationally expensive operations or complex parallelized execution plans will take more resources than the sample content queries used in the basic CPU sizing. Consequently, the CPU sizing has to be adapted accordingly.

In case that the query complexity of a customer scenario does not match or cannot be compared with the sample side-by-side scenario, throughput tests with customer specific data and queries have to be run to derive the sizing.

48. **Suppose you are building a multi host SAP HANA system with fail over capabilities then which of the following storage options are suitable?**
(There are three correct answers to the question)

(a) Using plain attached storage devices
(b) Standby host has file access
(c) Fencing should be taken care
(d) A shared storage subsystem is the commonly used storage option

Answer: b, c, d

Explanation:

In single-host SAP HANA systems, it is possible to use plain attached storage devices, such as SCSI hard drives, SSDs, or SANs. However, in order to build a multi-host system with failover capabilities, the storage must ensure the following:

- The standby host has file access.
- The failed worker host no longer has access to write to files - called fencing.

There are two fundamentally different storage configurations that meet the two conditions above: shared storage devices or separate storage devices with failover reassignment. A shared storage subsystem, such as NFS or IBM's GPFS, is the commonly used storage option because it is easy to ensure that the standby host has access to all active host files in the system.

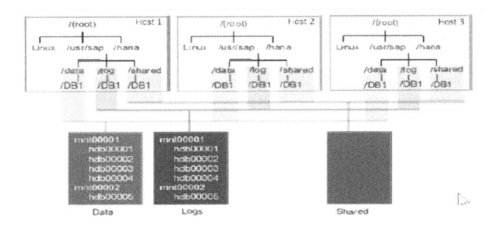

49. **What is RAM size equal to, in terms of table size and compression factor?**
    (Only one answer is correct)

    (a) (Table size & compression factor) + 2
    (b) (Table size & compression factor) × 2
    (c) (Table size & compression factor) / 2
    (d) (Table size & compression factor) - 2

Answer: b

Explanation:

Sizing SAP HANA

There are different factors for compression of data
- BW on SAP-HANA ~ fourfold (because BW has a significant part of his tables in the row store, only the application tables are in the column store and only these could be compressed).

- In the other use cases sevenfold

RAM Size = (Table size & compression factor) & 2
Table Size = (Size of table structure & number of records)

50. Which of the following is the general range of physical memory installed on most SAP HANA hosts?
(Only one answer is correct)

(a) 256 Kilobytes (KB) to 512 Kilobytes (KB)
(b) 256 Megabytes (MB) to 1 Gigabyte (GB)
(c) 1 Gigabyte (GB) to 10 Gigabytes (GB)
(d) 256 Gigabytes (GB) to 1 Terabyte (TB)

Answer: d

Explanation:

Virtual, Physical, and Resident Memory:

When (part of) the virtually allocated memory actually needs to be used, it is loaded or mapped to the real, physical memory of the host, and becomes "resident". Physical memory is the DRAM memory installed on the host.

On most SAP HANA hosts, it ranges from 256 Gigabytes (GB) to 1 Terabyte (TB). It is used to run the Linux operating system, SAP HANA and all other programs. Resident memory is the physical memory actually in operational use by a process.

51. Do write operations in column store directly modify the compressed data?
(Only one answer is correct)

(a) Yes
(b) No
(c) Always
(d) Mostly

Answer: b

Explanation:

Column Store
The column store uses efficient compression algorithms that help to keep all relevant application data in memory.
Write operations on this compressed data would be costly as they would require reorganizing the storage structure.
Therefore write operations in column store do not directly modify compressed data. All changes go into a separate area called the delta storage. The delta storage exists only in main memory. Only delta log entries are written to the persistence layer when delta entries are inserted.

52. **Suppose you have a requirement to create a multi host system then which of the following pre requisites should be taken into consideration?**
    (Only one answer is correct)

    (a) Shared file system for data files are configured
    (b) Shared file system for log files are configured
    (c) File system should be in mounted state
    (d) All of the above

Answer: d

Explanation:

Multi-Host System

A multi host system can be installed using SAP HANA lifecycle management tools with the below available options.

- Interactive mode
- Batch Mode
- Command Line or with the configuration file

Prerequisite
Shared file systems for the data files and log files are configured so that they are present and mounted on all hosts, including the primary host. The suggested locations for the file systems are as follows:
- /hana/shared
- /hana/data/<sid>
- /hana/log/<sid>

53. **Which of the following SAP Rapid Deployment Solutions provides maximum predictability and lowers the risk?**
    (Only one answer is correct)

(a) Services
(b) Software
(c) Enablement
(d) Content

Answer: a

Explanation:

Software
Quickly address the most urgent business processes

Content
SAP best practices, templates and tools make solution adoption easier

Enablement
Guides and educational material speed end user adoption

Service
Fixed scope and price provides maximum predictability and lowers risk

- With SAP Software, SAP Rapid Deployment solutions provide a ready-to-consume combination of SAP Predefined services, pre-configured content, and enablement content to accelerate the implementation and lower risk.
- Implementation is supported by standardized methodology and best practices, honed over decades. An optimized mix of global resources, remote support, and onsite consulting give you access to experts who can help you implement your solution on time and on budget.

54. **Which of the following actions will be performed when you migrate a single database to a multitenant database system?**
   (There are three correct answers to the question)

   (a) System database is generated
   (b) Tenant database is generated
   (c) Application data & customer data will be changed
   (d) No changes to application and customer data

Answer: a, b, d

Explanation:

The following actions will occur when you migrate a single database to multitenant database

- System database is generated
- Single database is converted into a tenant database automatically
- No changes to the application or customer data
- Migration must be explicitly triggered.

Conversion of Single database to multitenant database is an irrecoverable process.

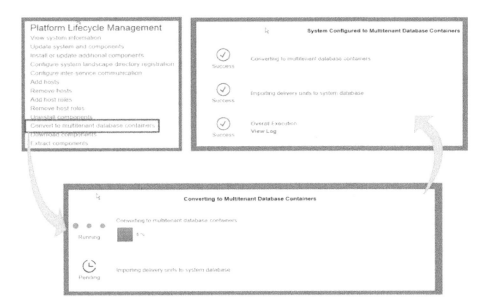

55. **Which of the following external interfaces allows client to connect and communicate with the SAP HANA Database?**
    (Only one answer is correct)

    (a) SQL
    (b) MDX
    (c) Web interface
    (d) All of the above

Answer: d

Explanation:

SAP HANA index server consists of several components that include various features as follows:
    • External Interfaces
    • Request Processing and Execution Control
    • Relational Engines
    • Storage Engine and Disk Storage

Structured Query Language (SQL), Multidimensional Expressions (MDX), and Web Interfaces allow clients to connect and communicate with the SAP HANA Database.

Simplified Architecture

- SAP HANA Core Process
- External Interfaces
  - Communicate with SAP HANA
  - Queries, Data Loads, Admin, ...
- Processing Engines
  - Operate on data
  - Execute Queries, ...
- Relational Engines
  - Store data (in Memory)
- Storage Engine
  - Handles data pages
  - Handles transfer RAM ⇔ Disk
- Disk Storage
  - Non-volatile data storage

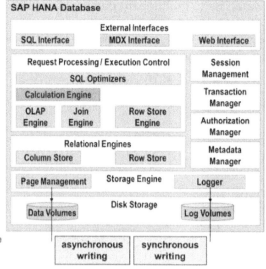

SAP HANA Installation and Upgrade

56. Which of the following parameters are required by the hardware partner prior to installation of SAP HANA?
(Only one answer is correct)

(a) Interface parameters
(b) SAP Application parameters
(c) Configuration parameters
(d) None of the above

Answer: c

Explanation:

- The installation of your SAP HANA appliance is performed by your hardware partner. Prior to installation your hardware partner needs information about configuration parameters like the SID or the hostname of your system.
- The components of SAP HANA and of the SAP HANA database can only be installed by certified hardware partners on validated hardware running a specific operating system. Any other system or content developed with such systems is not supported by SAP.

57. Which of the following are covered in SAP HANA appliance software from a deployment point of view?
(There are three correct answers to the question)

(a) SAP HANA platform edition
(b) SAP HANA internet
(c) SAP HANA client
(d) SAP HANA studio

Answer: a, c, d

Explanation:

The SAP HANA appliance software from a deployment point of view:

- SAP HANA platform edition
- SAP HANA database
- SAP HANA client
- SAP HANA studio
- SAP Host Agent

Additional components installed
- Machine readable product description
- SAP Software Update Manager for SAP HANA
- SAP Solution Manager Diagnostics Agent

- SAPCAR
- Operating System Configuration

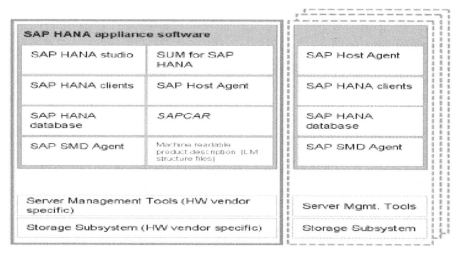

These are the core components of SAP HANA. This follows the SAP strategy to ship SL tools more asynchronous and release independent from products, but is covered by SAP HANA license bundle.

58. **Which of the following enables the customer or any SAP field specialist to download and implement new Support Package Stacks (SPS) and/or patches in an automated fashion from with HANA Studio?**
    (Only one answer is correct)

    (a) The Software Update Manager for SAP HANA
    (b) The SAP HANA on-site configuration tool
    (c) The SAP HANA unified installer
    (d) The SAP HANA agent

Answer: a

Explanation:

The SAP HANA unified installer: Enables the SAP Hardware Partner to pre-install all SAP HANA components in an effective and reproducible process.
The SAP HANA on-site configuration tool: Enables the Hardware vendor or any certified SAP field specialist to complete the system setup on-site the customer and adapt the factory defaults to the actual parameters suitable for the customer landscape.
The Software Update Manager for SAP HANA: Enables the customer or any SAP field specialist to download and implement new Support Package Stacks (SPS) and/or patches in an automated fashion from with HANA Studio.

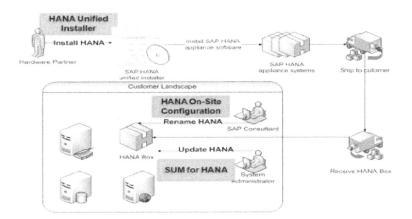

59. **Which of the following are the different steps there in Sizing of an SAP HANA System in Tailored data centre integration?**
(Only one answer is correct)

    (a) RAM Sizing
    (b) Disk Sizing
    (c) CPU sizing
    (d) All of the above

Answer: d

Explanation:

SAP HANA Tailored Data Centre Integration

Sizing of an SAP HANA Tailored Data Centre Integration consists of three main steps as follows

- RAM Sizing for static and dynamic data
- Disk Sizing for the persistence storage
- CPU Sizing for the queries and calculations

60. **Which of the following are calculated by SAP HANA Quick sizer tool?**
(There are three correct answers to the question)

    (a) CPU
    (b) Disk
    (c) Network Throughput
    (d) Memory

Answer: a, b, d

Explanation:

SAP HANA Database can be sized using Quick Sizer tool. The quick sizer calculates the following

- CPU
- Disk
- Memory
- Input/output resource categories

It calculates the above resources based on throughput numbers and the number of users working with the different SAP solutions in a hardware and database independent format.

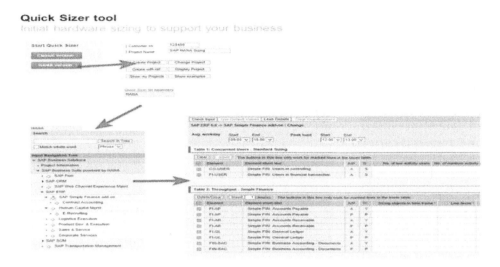

61. **What is the minimum space required for the Data volume?**
    (There are two correct answers to the question)

    (a) 1.2 * RAM (TDI)
    (b) Min 1* RAM
    (c) Min 0.5*RAM
    (d) 3*RAM (Appliance)

Answer: a, d

Explanation:

Disk Space required for the Data Volume

Whenever a save point or a snapshot, or perform a delta merge operation the data persists from the memory to the data volume under /hana/data/<SID>. For an SAP HANA System the recommended size of the data volume is equal to the calculated results from the sizing reports. Use the value on the disk plus an additional free space of 20%.

Below screenshot shows an example sizing report result for Suite on HANA. The sizing report shows the Net data size on the disk. To determine the required SAP HANA data volume sizes add 20%.

RESULTS OF SUITE ON HANA SIZING IN GB
Based on the selected table(s), the anticipated maximum memory requirement is
for Suite on HANA:

- Total memory requirement	2.412,3
- Net data size on disk	1.333,8

$$Size_{data} = 1.2x \text{ Net data size on disk}$$

Database Migration to SAP HANA

62. **Which of the following are the benefits of using DMO?**
    (Only one answer is correct)

    (a) Migration steps are simplified
    (b) Business downtime is reduced
    (c) SUM is used with improved UI
    (d) All of the above

Answer: d

Explanation:

With the classical migration option, you can migrate your existing ABAP based SAP system running on Any DB to HANA DB. But this involves complexity in performing the migration and also requires considering additional several steps.

To avoid this complexity, DMO of SUM tool offers the following benefits.

- Migration steps are simplified
- System update, Unicode Conversion and database migration are combined in one tool
- Business Downtime is reduced
- Well known tool SUM is used, with improved UI

63. **Which of the following are the prerequisites for DMO?**
    (Only one answer is correct)

    (a) Stack.xml file has to be created
    (b) Web browser update may have to be applied
    (c) OS/DB software update might required
    (d) All of the above

Answer: d

Explanation:

Below are the pre requisites for the DMO

- Dual-stack has to be split beforehand
- OS/DB software update may be required
- Stack.xml file has to be created using Maintenance Planner
- Web Browser update may have to be applied
- SAP BW: consider housekeeping, NLS, and BW-PCA

Dual-stack split only pure ABAP systems can be migrated onto the SAP HANA database. In case the system is a dual-stack system (both ABAP and Java stacks on one database, one System-ID); the dual-stack has to be split beforehand.

64. **Which of the following URL is being used to start the SUM for a DMO procedure by sending an appropriate HTTP request to the SAP Host Agent?**
    (Only one answer is correct)

    (a) http://<host>:<hostagentport>/lmls/sumabap/<SID>doc/gui
    (b) http://<host>:<hostagentport>/lmsl/sumabap/<SID>doc/gui
    (c) http://<host>:<hostagentport>/lmsl/
    (d) http://<host>:<hostagentport>/lmsl/SUM

Answer: a

Explanation:

The Software Update Manager (SUM) is the tool for system maintenance of SAP systems based on SAP Net Weaver. For the DMO procedure, a new way of starting the tool and a new user interface (UI) was introduced.

The following figure illustrates the different approach of the "classical" way of starting and using SUM compared to the DMO way of starting and using SUM.

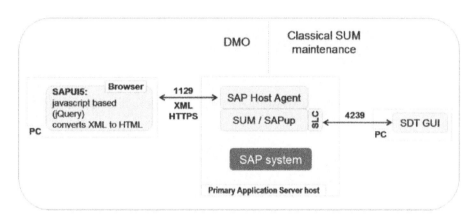

You use a browser window to start the SUM for a DMO procedure by sending an appropriate HTTP request to the SAP Host Agent. The URL that you use contains the information for the SAP Host Agent what to do. http://<host>:<hostagentnort>/lmsl/sumabap/<SID>doc/gui

- lmsl is the abbreviation for Lifecycle Management Software Logistics.
- <host> is the hostname of the primary application server of the source system
- <port> is the port of the SAP Host Agent (1129, or 1128 for plain HTTP)
- <SID> has to be replaced with the System-ID of the source system

65. **Which of the following are the features of DMO UI?**
    (Only one answer is correct)

(a) Standard functionality cannot be used with SAPUI5
(b) It is based on java script library
(c) Zero footprint, only browser
(d) All of the above

Answer: d

Explanation:

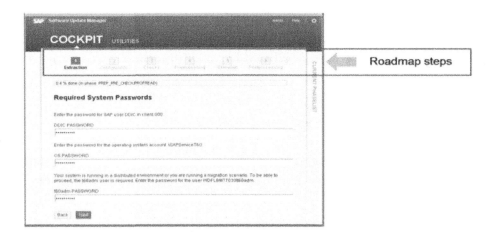

DMO UI
- SAPUI5 is an SAP library used in apps and offered for own development.
- The standard SUM functionality cannot be used with SAPUI5.
- SAPUI5 is based on a java script library (including jQuery).
- Benefit: zero footprint, only browser.

66. **Which of the following is the only difference in standard and advanced mode? (Only one answer is correct)**

(a) No of process assigned to the tools
(b) Downtime maintenance
(c) Complexity
(d) All of the above

Answer: a

Explanation:

Configuring DMO phase Configuration The roadmap step Configuration starts with the choice of the pre configuration mode.

The difference between Standard and Advanced mode is only the number of processes assigned to the tools.

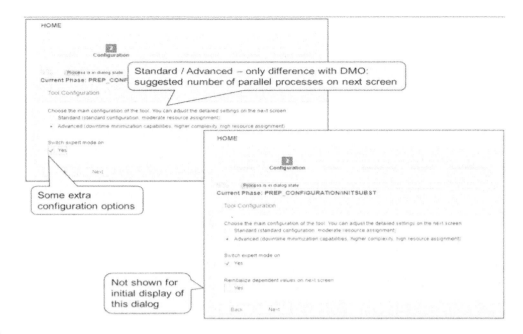

These numbers are maintained in the next dialog so you may choose pre configuration mode Standard, and then increase the number of processes to have the same values like Pre configuration mode Advanced.

67. **Suppose you want to migrate your existing SAP System from any DB to SAP HANA Database and had a requirement to reduce the business downtime and then which of the following option you will choose?**
(Only one answer is correct)

    (a) Update the application software and upgrade the database
    (b) In place migration option
    (c) Use DMO of SUM tool

(d) Update the application software, convert to Unicode and then upgrade to HANA DB

Answer: c

Explanation:

To migrate your existing SAP system from any DB to SAP HANA database you can choose the in place migration option to avoid landscape changes (SID, host name,), so you need an update of your SAP 7.x system. But this classical migration procedure is complex and requires several steps and tools.

To avoid this complexity use the database migration option (DMO) of Software Update Manager (SUM).

Benefits
- Migration steps are simplified
- System update and database migration are combined in one tool
- Business Downtime is reduced

DMO is not a new tool, it is just an option; a new option in an existing tool named Software Update Manager.

SUM is the trusted tool for system maintenance, such as:
- Release upgrades
- EHP implementations
- SP stacks for SAP Net Weaver-based systems

The "DMO Migration" is a one-step migration! This results in the following benefits. Upgrade and migration in a combined procedure reduces TCO and risks.

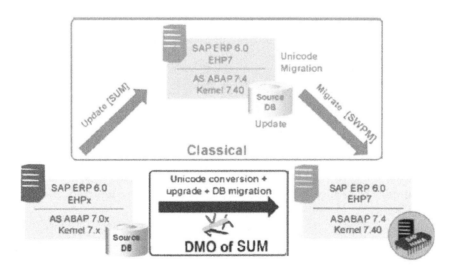

68. Which of the following are the possible reasons for the load/replication is stuck in scheduled state?

(There are three correct answers to the question)

(a) Mistake in IUUC_ASS_RUL_MAP table
(b) Mistake in IUUC_REPL_TABSTG table
(c) Syntax error in ABAP Include
(d) Mistake in IUUC_MAP Table

Answer: a, b, c

Explanation:

The possible reasons for the load/replication is stuck in the scheduled state are usually due to a transformation error on the SLT Replication Server.

Examples:
 * Typo or mistake in IUUC_ ASS_RUL_MAP table
 * Typo or mistake in IUUC_REPL_TABSTG table
 * Syntax error in an Include to be applied in the transformation this triggers an error flag in the affected table in the SLT Server monitor

To solve this issue, first check if the FAILED field is flagged by checking table dmc_mt_tables with transaction SE16.

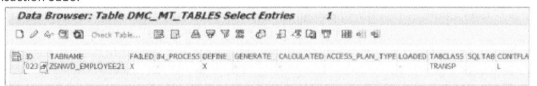

69. **Which of the following statements is true regarding the password change for the Replication Schema owner?**
    (There are three correct answers to the question)

    (a) Replication jobs which are running needs to be stopped
    (b) No change is required for currently running replication jobs
    (c) Password needs to be changed in multiple places if needed
    (d) You can change password in HANA System

Answer: a, c, d

Explanation:

It might be necessary to change the password of the schema owner of a target schema handled by LT Replication Server. As the password is also stored in the database connection in the SLT system, the password needs to be changed on both sides:
 * Stop any replication jobs (so that no jobs try to connect while the password is being changed).
 * Change the password in the HANA system

70. **Which of the following are the functionalities of the data integrator?**
    (Only one answer is correct)

    (a) Extract the data from the external sources
    (b) Transform the data
    (c) Data loading in data warehouse
    (d) All of the above

Answer: d

Explanation:

SAP Data Services enable you to gain deeper insight with a single, trusted view by accessing and integrating structured and unstructured data from data sources across your enterprise.
With data integrator you can Extract, transform, and load data into a data warehouse.

- SAP HANA repository support
- SAP HANA performance improvements
- Bulk updates enhancement Support for stored procedures
- Data streaming in ABAP data flows
- SAP table reader in regular data flows
- Parallel reading from business content extractors
- New ABAP functions for improved security

71. **Which of the following BW objects facilitates the actual movement of data through the ETL process?**
    (There are two correct answers to the question)

    (a) Info Packages
    (b) Info Providers
    (c) Data Sources
    (d) Data Transfer Process

Answer: a, d

Explanation:

- The basic BW Data Flow is the process of taking data from a source system, applying transformation rules to it, and loading it to a BW Info Provider (data target).
- Info Packages and the Data Transfer Processes are the SAP BW objects that facilitate the actual movement of data through the ETL process.
- Info Packages load data from the Source System to the PSA without any transformation.
- Info Packages and Data Transfer Processes should be included into a Process Chain to automate the loading process.

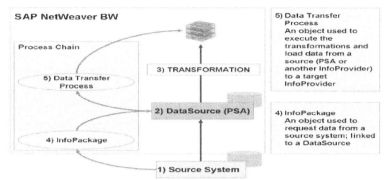

72. **Which of the following methods provided by Data Services for moving data into and out of SAP Applications?**
(Only one answer is correct)

(a) Data Exchange via RFC
(b) ABAP Programming language
(c) RFC/BAPI
(d) All of the above

Answer: d

Explanation:

Data Services provides several methods for moving data into and out of SAP applications:

Data exchange via RFC: It reads data from SAP applications using regular data flows and supports tables and extractors.
ABAP programming language: Reads data from SAP applications using ABAP data flows and supports tables, hierarchies, extractors, and functions with scalar arguments.
RFC/BAPI: It loads data to SAP applications and allows direct access to application tables outside of the data flows through RFC function calls.
Idoc interface: Reads from and loads data to SAP applications. Data Services can send, receive, and create custom Idoc and supports reduced input sets, parallel processing, real-time, and batch processing.

73. **Which of the following statements are true regarding Data Services?**
(Only one answer is correct)

(a) Data Services supports HANA Database as repository host
(b) Data Services automatically detects the HANA target table type
(c) It can be used as transparent staging table for bulk loading to targets
(d) All of the above

Answer: d

Explanation:

SAP HANA repository support Data Services now supports the SAP HANA database as a repository host. It is not required to use a separate database to host the Data Services repository.

SAP HANA performance improvements

Data Services automatically detects the SAP HANA target table type and updates the table accordingly for optimal performance.

Bulk updates enhancement

Data Services now uses a transparent staging table for bulk loading to targets for improved performance when using changed-data capture or auto-correct load.

Support for stored procedures

Data Services now supports SAP HANA stored procedures. Scalar data types are supported for input and output parameters. Procedures can be called from a script or a Query transform as a new function call.

74. **Which of the following is used by DXC to handle the extremely challenging proper application logic to implement on a project basis in SAP HANA?**
    (Only one answer is correct)

    (a) Using Extractors
    (b) By implementing the logic from scratch
    (c) Using In memory data store objects
    (d) None of the above

    Answer: a

    Explanation:

    Challenges
    - In many modules of SAP Business Suite systems → Application logic needed to have semantically rich data (data appropriately reflecting the state of business documents)
    - LT "real-time" approach → uses base tables in the SAP Business Suite as a basis for data modeling → semantically rich data not provided "out of the box"

    Project solution:
    - Implement business logic from scratch to properly represent SAP Business Suite data.
    - It can be extremely challenging to determine proper application logic to implement on a project basis in SAP HANA.

    DXC Benefits
    - DXC → uses SAP Data Source Extractors →provides semantically rich data "out of the box" Ensures the data appropriately represents the state of business documents from ERP Application logic to "make sense of the data" already built into many extractors.
    - Avoid potentially difficult work of "reinventing the wheel" on a project basis in HANA → re implement application logic in NANA which is already provided in Data Source extractors.

75. **Which of the following statements is true regarding the Business Content Data Source Extractors?**
    (Only one answer is correct)

    (a) Extractors are application based

(b) Extractors is even driven technology
(c) It can be easily enhanced
(d) All of the above

Answer: d

Explanation:

- Extractors are application based and take data from the context of the application itself.
- Extraction is event/process driven and (in some cases) is accomplished with publishing new or changed data in ERP based Delta Queues for receiving systems
- Transformations can be implemented at the time of extraction using Business Add Ins (BADIs) Extract Structures based on entities in the Business Suite Asynchronous, mass data capable extraction

76. **Which of the following are the benefits of the HANA Optimized Info Cubes as compared to standard Info cubes?**
    (Only one answer is correct)

    (a) Fast Data Loads
    (b) Faster structural changes
    (c) Multi providers remain unchanged
    (d) All of the above

Answer: d

Explanation:

Benefits: Fast data loads up to 80% time reduction Dimensions not physically present for simpler modeling and faster structural changes.
All processes, all Queries and Multi Providers can remain unchanged.

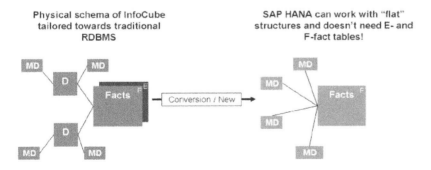

77. **Which of the following field is required for Optimizing SAP HANA and is hidden in queries?**
    (Only one answer is correct)

    (a) RECORDMODE
    (b) SOURSYSTEM

(c) IMO_INT_KEY

(d) DOC_NUMBER

Answer: c

Explanation:

SAP HANA Optimized Data Store objects contain the additional field IMO_INT_KEY in the active data table. This field is required for optimizing SAP HANA and is hidden in queries.

78. **Which of the following scenarios exist for the landscape reorganization of SAP HANA database during DMO?**
    (There are two correct answers to the question)

    (a) Horizontal distribution
    (b) Scale up
    (c) Scale Out
    (d) Vertical distribution

Answer: b, c

Explanation:

Landscape reorganization for SAP HANA DB
Landscape reorganization for SAP HANA DB is required during DMO; it partitions and distributes the tables across SAP HANA nodes.

There are two scenarios exist for the Landscape reorganization and it depends on number of existing SAP HANA nodes: scale up (only one node) and scale out (several nodes, currently only supported for SAP BW)
Scale-out: After selection of this check box another dialog is shown before the table creation, asking you to import a file to SAP HANA. SAP up later triggers the distribution of the tables across SAP HANA Nodes.

Scale Up: Do not select this checkbox. Prior to UT migration a dialog is shown asking you to manually import a file for the table partitioning for tables more than 2 million entries.

79. **Which of the following folders are relevant for monitoring and troubleshooting during migration procedure?**
    (Only one answer is correct)

    (a) Htdoc
    (b) Log
    (c) Srv
    (d) All of the above

Answer: d

Explanation:

The following folders are relevant for monitoring and troubleshooting (all folders under sum\abap\):
Folders for Monitoring and Troubleshooting
log
Log files (same as UI section logs).
For example, error logs, SAPupConsole.log. SAPupStats.log
tmp
Temporary files, especially SAPupDialog.txt
If a dialog is open (not for roadmap switches)
srv
HTTP log files of SAPup (gt=httpchannel)
htdoc
UPGANA.XML file contains information like timing, component level, and much more.

80. **Which of the following different options available in DMO tool for changing the process parameters during runtime?**
    (There are three correct answers to the question)
    (a) Using SUM Utilities
    (b) Using URL provided by SAP
    (c) Using Command Prompt
    (d) Using a Background job

Answer: a, b, c

Explanation:

Changing process parameters during Runtime

- Use the More/Utilities menu and choose SUM Parameters/ Process Parameters. A new browser window displays called Software Update Manager Utilities

- Access via a browser in a separate window
  http://<host>:1128/lmsl/sumabap/<SID>/set/procpar

- User the command prompt to start new SAPup:
    SAPup set procpar gt=scroll

For all three ways: the SAPupParameterConsole.log log is written.

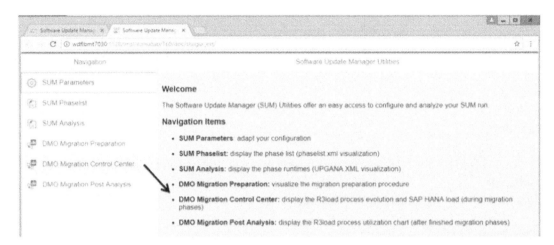

81. **Which of the following actions are still possible after confirming Lock now option in the DMO tool?**
    (Only one answer is correct)

    (a) Developing via ABAP workbench (SE80)
    (b) Applying SAP Note via Note Assistant
    (c) Creating and changing application data(e.g., VA01) and user master records(SU01)
    (d) Releasing and importing transport requests via the Transport Manager(SE09) and Transport Management System(STMS)

Answer: c

Explanation:

You cannot use the ABAP workbench, cannot use the Note Assistant, and cannot release and import the transport requests. But you can still change application data and user master records

High Availability and Disaster Recovery

82. **Which of the following different levels of defense against failure related outages provided by SAP HANA?**
    (There are two correct answers to the question)

    (a) Hardware Redundancy
    (b) Memory Redundancy
    (c) Database Redundancy
    (d) Persistence

Answer: a, d

Explanation:

The key to achieving high availability is redundancy, including hardware redundancy, network redundancy, and data center redundancy. SAP HANA provides several levels of defense against failure related outages:

Hardware Redundancy
SAP HANA appliance vendors offer multiple layers of redundant hardware, software, and network components, such as redundant power supplies and fans, enterprise grade error-correcting memories, fully redundant network switches and routers, and uninterrupted power supplies (UPS).

Software
SAP HANA is based on SUSE Linux Enterprise 11 for SAP and includes security pre configurations (for example, minimal network services). Additionally, the SAP HANA system software also includes a watchdog function, which automatically restarts configured services (index server, name server, and so on), in case of detected stoppage (killed or crashed).

Persistence
SAP HANA persist transaction logs, save points, and snapshots to support system restart and recovery from host failures, with minimal delay and without loss of data.

Standby and Failover
Separate, dedicated standby hosts are used for failover, in case of failure of the primary, active hosts. This improves the availability by significantly reducing the recovery time from an outage.

83. **Which of the following are the different ways SAP HANA is supported for distributing data between multiple indexes servers in a single system?**
    (There are two correct answers to the question)

    (a) Index partitioning
    (b) Database partitioning
    (c) Table partitioning
    (d) Row partitioning

Answer: b, c

Explanation:

Data Distribution: SAP HANA supports different ways of distributing data between multiple index servers in a single system:

- Different tables can be assigned to different index servers, which normally run on different hosts (database partitioning).
- A table can be split in a way that different rows of the table are stored on different index servers (table partitioning).

When a non-partitioned table is created in a distributed system, it must be assigned to one index server. By default, new tables are distributed across available index servers using a round-robin approach. For example, if there are three available index servers A, B, and C (including the master), the first table created will be located on server A, the next one on server B, the next on server C, and so on.

84. **Which of the following is the drawback of using backup as disaster recovery support? (Only one answer is correct)**

    (a) Loss of index
    (b) Loss of data
    (c) Loss of hardware
    (d) Loss of Network

Answer: b

Explanation:

Storage Replication
One drawback of backups is the potential loss of data between the time of the last backup and the time of the failure. Therefore, a preferred solution is to provide continuous replication of all persisted data. Several SAP HANA hardware partners offer a storage-level replication solution, which delivers a backup of the volumes or file system to a remote, networked storage system.

85. **Which of the following factors causes performance impact on using storage replication? (Only one answer is correct)**

    (a) Distance between data centers
    (b) Connection between data centers
    (c) Latency
    (d) All of the above

Answer: d

Explanation:

Storage Replication Performance impact is to be expected on data changing operations as soon as the synchronous mirroring is activated. The impact depends strongly on various external factors like distance, connection between data centers, and so on. The synchronous writing of the log with the concluding COMMITS is the crucial part here.

In case of an emergency, the primary data center is not available anymore and a process for the take-over must be initiated. This take-over process then would end the mirroring officially, will mount the disks to the already installed SAP HANA software and instances, and start up the secondary database side of the cluster.

86. **Which of the following different replication modes available for HANA disaster recovery? (There are two correct answers to the question)**

    (a) Sync
    (b) Half sync
    (c) Full sync
    (d) Sync data

Answer: a, c

Explanation:

Synchronous (replication Mode=sync)
The primary system does not commit a transaction until it receives confirmation that the log has been persisted in the secondary system. This mode guarantees immediate consistency between both systems, however, the transaction is delayed by the time it takes to transmit the data to and persist it in the secondary system.

Synchronous (replication Mode= Full Sync)
Log write is successful, when the log buffer has been written to the log volume of the primary and the secondary instance. In addition, when the secondary system is getting disconnected (e g. because of network failures), the primary systems suspends transaction processing until the connection to the secondary system is re-established. No data loss occurs in this scenario.

87. **Which of the following is the suitable option for overcoming the hardware limitations of a single physical server? (Only one answer is correct)**

    (a) Scale up
    (b) Scale out
    (c) Scale in
    (d) All of the above

Answer: b

Explanation:

There are two general approaches to scale your SAP HANA system

Scale up: It means increasing the size of one physical machine by increasing the amount of physical resources like RAM, CPU available for processing.

Scale out: It means combining multiple computers into one system. The main reason for distributing the system across multiple hosts is to overcome the limitations of a single physical server. This means an SAP HANA system can be distribute the load between multiple servers.

Scale-up (scale vertically)
- Increase the size of the hardware (main memory, number of CPUs)
- Challenge:
    - Availability of suitable hardware

Scale-out (scale horizontally)
- Several nodes (servers) are switched together for one database
- Data is distributed over the main memories of these different nodes
- Challenge:
    - Cross-node communication is expensive:
      Avoid cross-node joins / views
    - Table distribution has to be customer / usage pattern specific
    - Dynamic redistribution must be allowed

88. **SAP HANA is offered in the following ways?**
    (Only one answer is correct)

    (a) On premise appliance
    (b) Tailored data centre model
    (c) Cloud based service
    (d) All of the above

Answer: d

Explanation:

SAP HANA is offered in several ways. It is offered in the form of

- On premise appliance with number of different configurations and sizes
- As a tailored data centre integration model
- Cloud-based service

This creates different design options for scale up and scale out variants. To maximize the performance and throughput scale up the system as far as possible before scale out. So it is suggested to acquire the highest processor and memory configuration for the application workloads and scale out for deployments for greater data volume requirements.

89. **Which of the following statements are true regarding data distribution using SAP BW/4 HANA?**

    (Only one answer is correct)

    (a) Tables are partitioned distributed between nodes
    (b) Distribution works well in static environment
    (c) OLAP load benefits from parallel processing of queries
    (d) All of the above

Answer: d

Explanation:

Data distribution with SAP BW/4 HANA

- Tables are partitioned and the partitions are distributed over the different nodes.
- Distribution works well in the static environment such as Fact, Data Store Object, and PSA tables in SAP BW but not within SAP Business Suite.
- OLAP load benefits from parallel processing of queries.
- Sizing of SAP HANA for BW offers detailed information about the size of row and column store.

Backup and Recovery

90. Which of the following are the functions of log in SAP HANA database?
(Only one answer is correct)

(a) Information about data changes (redo log)
(b) Directly saved to persistent storage when transaction is committed
(c) Cyclical overwrite (only after backup)
(d) All of the above

Answer: d

Explanation:

SAP HANA database holds the bulk of its data in memory to ensure optimal performance. However, it still uses persistent storage to provide a fallback in case of failure.
Data:
- SQL data and undo log information
- Additional HANA information, such as modeling data
- Kept in-memory to ensure maximum performance
- Write process is asynchronous

Log:
- Information about data changes (redo log)
- Directly saved to persistent storage when transaction is committed
- Cyclical overwrite (only after backup)

91. Which of the following option is correct to protect database against data loss due to disk failures?
(Only one answer is correct)

(a) Save points
(b) Logs
(c) Backups
(d) Memory

Answer: b

Explanation:

During normal database operation, data is automatically saved from memory to disk at regular save points. Additionally, all data changes are recorded in the redo log. The redo log is saved from memory to disk with each committed database transaction. After a power failure, the database can be restarted like any disk-based database, and it returns to its consistent state by replaying the redo log since the last save point.

While save points and log writing protect your data against power failures, save points do not help if the persistent storage itself is damaged. To protect against data loss due to disk failures, backups are required. Backups save the payload (the actual data) of the data area and log area to different locations. Currently only backups to the file system are supported.

Backups are performed while the database is running. The impact of backups on system performance is negligible, and users can continue to work normally while the backup is running.

92. **Which of the following data can be backed up and restored using backups?**
    (There are two correct answers to the question)

    (a) Data area
    (b) Configuration files
    (c) Log area
    (d) Minute changes

Answer: a, c

Explanation:

Database should be backed up to avoid data loss due to disk failures. Database backup included back up of:

- Data area – from persistent storage to external backup locations
- Log area – is backed up automatically
- Configuration files (.ini files) – could be backed up manually

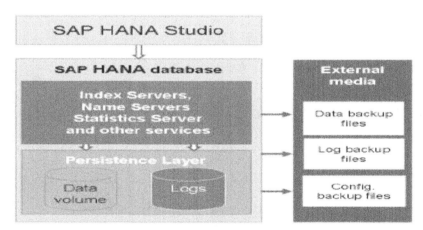

93. **Which of the following functions are provided by BACKINT for SAP HANA?**
    (Only one answer is correct)

    (a) Check
    (b) Recovery
    (c) Query
    (d) Delete

Answer: a

Explanation:

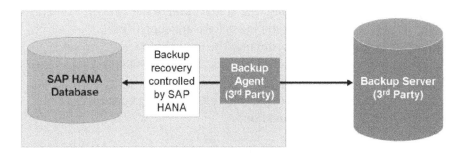

"BACKINT for SAP HANA" is an API that can be implemented by a 3rd party backup agent.

- Provides functions for backup, recovery, query, and delete
- 3rd party backup agents runs on SAP HANA server and communicates with 3rd party backup server
- Backups are transferred through pipes.
- Full integration with SAP HANA studio (configuration and execution of backups to BACKINT).
- BACKINT can be configured both for data backups and for log backups.

94. Which of the following displays actions that are scheduled to run in the background? (Only one answer is correct)

(a) DBA Planning Cockpit
(b) SQL Cockpit
(c) SAL DBA Planner
(d) DBA Planning Calendar

Answer: d

Explanation:

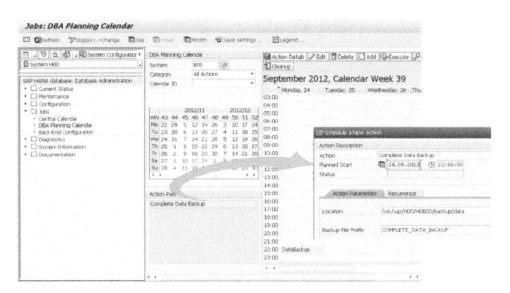

DBA Planning Calendar:
- Can be used to schedule, execute, and check almost all regular database administration actions.
- The scheduled actions are executed automatically.
- Displays actions that are scheduled to run in the background.
- To start DBA Cockpit, use transaction code DBACOCKPIT.

95. **Which of the following option has to be specified when the action will be repeated or whether it will be executed only once?**
    (Only one answer is correct)

    (a) DBA Planning Calendar
    (b) Recurrence
    (c) Planned Start
    (d) Action parameters

Answer: b

Explanation:

Below are the steps to be followed for scheduling the backups using DBA planning calendar.

- In DBA Cockpit, choose: Jobs → DBA Planning Calendar
- To create a new action, you can do either of the following:
    ✓ Double-click a calendar row.
    ✓ Select a calendar cell and choose Add
- Drag and drop on action from the Action Pad to a calendar cell in the future. You can also drag and drop actions reschedule them
- To copy an action, hold down the CTRL key while dragging.
- Specify the action details:
    ✓ Planned Start – Specify the start date and time of the action
    ✓ Action Parameters – If different from the default, specify the location and prefix for the file.
    ✓ Recurrence – Specify when the action will be repeated or whether it will be executed only once.

96. **Which of the following authorizations are required to perform the operations related to backup and recovery?**
    (Only one answer is correct)

    (a) BACKUP ADMIN
    (b) BACKUP OPERATOR
    (c) CATALOG READ
    (d) All of the above

Answer: d

Explanation:

To perform operations related to backup and recovery, the following authorizations are required:

Task	Required authorizations
Backup	• BACKUP ADMIN or BACKUP OPERATOR • CATALOG READ This privilege is required in order to collect the information needed by the backup wizard
Recover	The recovery process is executed as the operating system user (<sid>adm). You must therefore have the logon credentials of this user.
Open the Backup editor	•BACKUP ADMIN • CATALOG READ
Delete data and log backups from the backup catalog and physically from the backup location	BACKUP ADMIN

97. **Which of the following system privilege can help the user to delete the backup configurations?**
    (Only one answer is correct)

    (a) BACKUP ADMIN
    (b) CATALOG READ
    (c) BACKUP OPERATOR
    (d) Both a & c

Answer: a

Explanation:

A user with the system privilege BACKUP ADMIN can perform all backup-related operations, including backup deletion and configuration.
A user with the system privilege BACKUP OPERATOR can only perform backups.
For example, if you have automated the regular performance of backups using cron, it is more secure to use a user with the privilege BACKUP OPERATOR to avoid the malicious deletion of backups.

98. **Which of the following different options available for carrying out backups for SAP HANA?**
    (Only one answer is correct)

    (a) Backups to file system
    (b) Backups via BACKINT interface
    (c) Data Snapshots using storage tools
    (d) All of the above

Answer: d

Explanation:

Data backups and log backups for SAP HANA system can be written to the file system or any third party backup tools which are supported by SAP.

The BACKINT for SAP HANA interface performs all the actions needed to write the backup data to external storage. The backup tools communicate directly with the SAP HANA database through the BACKINT for SAP HANA interface.

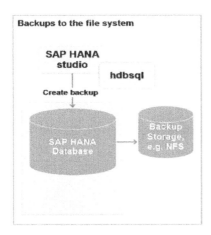 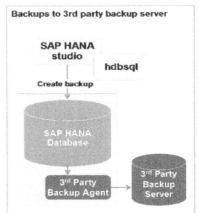

99. **Data backups can be triggered using the following?**
    (Only one answer is correct)

    (a) SAP HANA Cockpit
    (b) SAP HANA Studio
    (c) SQL Commands
    (d) All of the above

Answer: d

Explanation:

Data backups for SAP HANA database can be performed using the following tools.

*   **SAP HANA Studio:** Click on Choose Backup and specify the backup locations or use the default destination specified in the parameter.
*   **SAP HANA Cockpit:** You can use the app manage database backups in SAP HANA cockpit.
*   **SQL Commands:** You can enter SQL commands either by using SQL editor in HANA studio or using hdbsql program in the command line.

100.   **Which of the following is the typical size of the area for log volume?**
        (Only one answer is correct)

(a) Twice the main memory of HANA
(b) One time the main memory of HANA
(c) Three times the main memory of HANA
(d) Equals to main memory of HANA

Answer: b

Explanation:

Log writing
- Log is written to Log-Buffers in Memory
- Log backup saves log information out of the log segments into log backup files; the log segment files are not deleted in file system (Log mode = normal)
- Backed up log segments files are defined as empty and re-consumed for new log segments (no reallocation on file system needed) Typical sizing of the area for Log volume
- One times main memory of HANA node

101. In which of the following mode you can recover the database to a specific backup? (Only one answer is correct)

(a) Normal
(b) Circular
(c) Overwrite
(d) Legacy

Answer: c

Explanation:

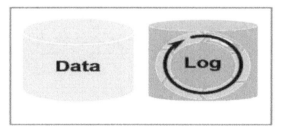

With log_mode = overwrite, no point-in-time recovery is possible. For recovery, only data backups are used; the logs are not used.
Only the following recovery option can be selected:
- Recover the database to a specific data backup
- This can be useful, for example, for test installations that do not need to be backed up or recovered.
- log_mode = overwrite is not recommended for production systems.

102.   **Which of the following information backup catalog includes?**
        (Only one answer is correct)

(a) An external backup ID
(b) Volumes that were backed up
(c) Backup destination and their sizes
(d) All of the above

Answer: d

Explanation:

The backup catalog includes the following information:
- Backups performed for a database
- The start and finish times of the backups
- Whether a backup is still running
- Whether a backup was successful or not
- Volumes that were backed up
- Log backups and what part of the log they contain
- Backup destinations and their sizes
- Whether the redo log history was interrupted
- The destination type
- An external backup ID

103.   **Which of the following contains information regarding data pages and before images?**
        (Only one answer is correct)

(a) Log volumes
(b) Data volumes
(c) Redo log entries
(d) Page log entries

Answer: b

Explanation:

- Redo log entries are written to log volumes at latest when a transaction ends changed data itself is written at latest when a save point is performed.
- Data pages and undo log pages are written on the data volumes. After images (redo log pages) are written on the log volumes.

Monitoring and troubleshooting of SAP HANA

104. In which of the following system EWA session will be executed?
(Only one answer is correct)

(a) Solman
(b) HANA DB server
(c) S/4 HANA system
(d) All of the above

Answer: a

Explanation:

Below are the step by step details for executing the EWA session

- Batch job triggers data collection on HANA database server via Host Agent.
- Host Agent starts data collection Script.
- Information is passed back to background job.
- Results in background job are collected in SDCC and sent to Solman.
- EWA session is executed on Solman and EWA report is created.

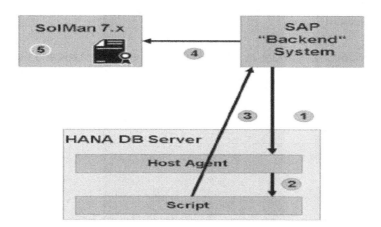

105. Which of the following are not covered in terms of Size and Growth?
(Only one answer is correct)

(a) Volume Files
(b) System Configuration
(c) Data Volume Size
(d) Tables and Indexes

Answer: b

Explanation:

Disk Usage
- Separated in Data / Anchor / Log file

Size of Volume Files
- Size of Volume files separated by different services

Table and Indexes
- Number of Columnar and Row Store Tables
- Indexes of Row Store tables
- Size of Row and Column Store Tables

The Size and Growth contains:
- Volume Files (Separated by Data / Log / Trace Files)
- Disk Usage (Separated by Partitions)
- Data Volume Size (separated by files belonging to the services)
- Tables and Indexes

106.   **Which of the following privileges are required to redistribute tables across the hosts in your system?**
         (There are two correct answers to the question)

(a) RESOURCE ADMIN
(b) DISTRIBUTE
(c) ALTER
(d) FILTER

Answer: a, c

Explanation:

Tables can be redistributed across the hosts in your system and to perform this action a privilege RESOURCE ADMIN and at least the object privilege ALTER all schemas is required. As redistributing the data is a critical operation it is recommended to save the current distribution so you can restore it if necessary.

After the system marks the host for removal and executes the required redistribution operation, the data on the index server of the host being moved to the index servers of the remaining hosts in the system. The redistribution operation appears in the list of executed operations on the Redistribution tab.

107.   **Which of the following statement helps in activating the expensive statement trace in HANA?**
         (Only one answer is correct)

(a) By entering a threshold for the statement runtime
(b) By not entering a threshold for the statement runtime
(c) By entering a threshold for the system runtime
(d) By not entering a threshold for the system runtime

Answer: a

Explanation:

Statement Monitoring

- The SQL Plan Cache automatically collects statistics about statement execution.
- The runtime statistics are aggregated for all executions of the same statement.
- The statistics collection can be disabled.
- The Expensive Statements Trace needs to be activated by entering a threshold for the statement runtime. Afterwards all statements exceeding the specified runtime are logged

108. **Which of the following enables the user to analyze problems which might occur during the start/stop phase of the SAP HANA database and to read diagnosis files even when the database is stopped?**
    (Only one answer is correct)

    (a) Collection of information about the SAP HANA installer using the sapstartsrv connection by SAP HANA studio
    (b) Collection of information about the SAP HANA database using the sapstopsrv connection by SAP HANA studio
    (c) Collection of information about the SAP HANA database using the sapstartsrv connection by SAP HANA database
    (d) Collection of information about the SAP HANA database using the sapstartsrv connection by SAP HANA studio

Answer: d

Explanation:

Diagnosis Mode for Administration Editor
- Provides information available without SQL connection (using sapstartsrv)
- Displays service list with detailed status of services during start/stop phase
- Provides access to diagnosis files.

109. **Which of the following is the general sequence of updating the SAP HANA Components?**
    1. **Make a system backup**
    2. **Stop all process**
    3. **Update the dependent components**
    4. **Perform an update**
    5. **Perform the post update**
    6. **Restart all process**
    (Only one answer is correct)

    (a) 1,2,3,4,5,6
    (b) 2,3,1,4,5,6
    (c) 2,1,4,3,5,6

Page **74** of **97**

(d) 6,4,3,2,1,5

Answer: c

Explanation:

The Update Process Before updating the SAP HANA components, make sure that no read or write processes are running on the SAP HANA database. Perform the update process in offline mode during a business downtime. After the update, you have to start SAP HANA and its components again.

There is a general sequence of the steps you have to perform.

- Stop all processes.
- Make a system backup if necessary.
- Perform an update.
- Update the depending components.
- Perform the post-update steps.
- Restart all processes.

110. **Which of the following files provides a delta analysis of the original trace files and makes detailed analysis easier?**
    (Only one answer is correct)

    (a) <hdbcommand>.log
    (b) <hdbcommand>.msg
    (c) <hostname>_tracediff.tgz
    (d) All of the above

Answer: c

Explanation:

The SAP HANA lifecycle management tools hdblcm and hdblcmgui write log files during installation. The most recent log file is always available under /var/tmp/hdblcm.log or /var/tmp/hdblcmgui.log

The following files are written while performing the action

<hdbcommand.log>: can be read using text editor
<hdbcommand.msg>: XML format for the display in the installation tool with SAP GUI
<hostname>_tracediff.tgz: Provides a delta analysis of the original trace files and makes detailed analysis easier.

111. **Which page displays a list of all hosts belonging to the specific HANA database as well as the configured and current role of the corresponding services?**
    (Only one answer is correct)

a. Landscape tab page
b. Services tab page
c. Configuration tab page
d. None of the above

Answer: c

Explanation:

The Configuration tab page displays a list of all hosts belonging to the specific HANA database as well as the configured and current role of the corresponding services.
It is also possible to change the roles of the services to reconfigure the high availability scenario.

112. **What does it mean when the overview tab under General Information indicates yellow?**
    (Only one answer is correct)

    (a) All services are active and in sync
    (b) All services are active, but not in sync yet
    (c) Errors in replication
    (d) All services are not active but in sync

Answer: b

Explanation:

The Overview tab under General Information shows the status of the Secondary System Replication:
- Green – all services are active and in sync
- Yellow – all services are active but not in sync yet
- Red – errors in replication

113. **Which of the following is the correct path for the table redistribution in SAP HANA?**
    (Only one answer is correct)

    (a) Landscape →System →Redistribution
    (b) System →Settings→ Redistribution
    (c) Settings →Distribution →Redistribution

(d) Landscape →Configuration →Redistribution

Answer: d

Explanation:

User Interface for Table Redistribution: In the Administration editor, choose Landscape →Configuration →Redistribution.
There are several redistribution operations available to support the following situations:
- You are planning to remove a host from your system
- You have added a new host to your system
- You want to optimize current table distribution
- You want to optimize table partitioning

114.   **Which of the following is to be done before you can remove a host from your SAP HANA database system?**
(Only one answer is correct)

(a) The tables on the index server of the host in question should be moved to the index servers on the remaining hosts in the system.
(b) The tables on the system server of the host in question should be moved to the servers on the remaining hosts in the system.
(c) The tables on the host in question should be moved to the remaining hosts in the system.
(d) The tables on the index server of the host in question should be moved to the index servers on the remaining hosts in the system.

Answer: d

Explanation:

Remove host from landscape
Below are the high level steps to be followed for removing the host from landscape

- In the Administration editor, choose Landscape →Configuration
- From the context menu of the host that you plan to remove, choose Remove Host
- In the Remove Host dialog box, choose yes
- The system marks the host for removal and executes the required redistribution operation

Before you can remove a host from your SAP HANA database system, you must move the tables on the index server of the host in question to the index servers on the remaining hosts in the system. To be able to redistribute tables across the hosts in your system, you must have the system privilege RESOURCE ADMIN and at least the object privilege ALTER for all schemas involved.

115. **Is operating system user authentication required when restarting the database?**
(Only one answer is correct)

(a) Yes
(b) No
(c) Never
(d) Sometimes

Answer: a

Explanation:

Database Restart: Starting and stopping the database is possible via the context menu in the Navigator. Operating system user authentication required.
In the Navigator open the context menu on the database entry and choose either Start or Restart. After confirming the (re)start, you need to enter the operating system user and password, before the database is actually restarted. It is possible to store the operating system user credentials in the Eclipse secure store. This enables you to run actions which require authentication with this user without entering the credentials each time.

116. **Which of the following events can trigger an event on the Overview tab of the Administration editor in addition to the bar view of the disk usage?**
(Only one answer is correct)

(a) If the storage on which database files are stored is empty
(b) If the storage on which database files are stored is exactly half-filled
(c) If the storage on which database files are stored runs full
(d) If the storage on which database files are stored is not full

Answer: c

Explanation:

Disk Full Handling: If the storage on which database files are stored runs full, the database gets suspended and an event is triggered. This event is displayed on the Overview tab of the Administration editor in addition to the bar view of the disk usage.
The disk full situation has to be resolved (additional storage space has to be provided or unused files to be deleted) AND the event has to be marked as handled before the database can resume its work.

117. **Which of the following page provides a graphical view of memory consumption?**

(Only one answer is correct)

(a) Performance tab page
(b) Threads tab page
(c) Load tab page
(d) Quality tab page

Answer: c

Explanation:

- On the performance tab page, information about running threads and performance KPIs is displayed.
- The threads tab page displays a list of all threads and their status- filters can be applied.
- The Load tab page provides a graphical view of specific performance KPIs (like CPU usage, memory consumption, etc.).

118.   How do you know that threads are blocked?
(Only one answer is correct)

(a) They are deleted
(b) They are highlighted
(c) They are ignored
(d) They are hidden

Answer: b

Explanation:

Blocking Situations:
Blocking situations are visualized – blocked threads are highlighted.
A blocked thread is marked with a warning icon and the tooltip provides detailed information.
As for most views in SAP HANA studio one can add further columns to the view – e.g. the transaction ID, which might be interesting in case of a blocking situation.

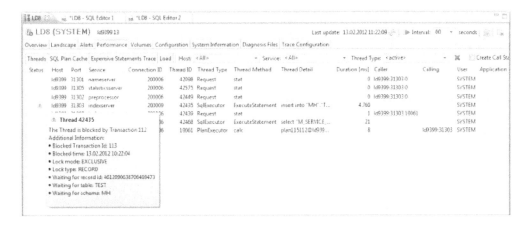

119.   If the operation of a specific thread is ended in a session/transaction, what happens to other threads belonging to that session/transaction?
(Only one answer is correct)

(a) The operations of all other threads belonging to that session/transaction will be ended as well.
(b) The operations of all other threads belonging to that session/transaction will continue as they are.
(c) The operations of some threads belonging to that session/transaction will be ended as well.
(d) The operations of all other threads belonging to that session/transaction will not be affected.

Answer: a

Explanation:

Cancel Operations: All threads belonging to the specific session are canceled as the complete session/transaction needs to be canceled.

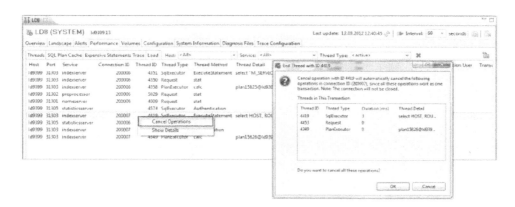

In the Thread View it is now possible to end the operation of a specific thread. As several threads run together in one session and in one transaction, the operations of all other threads belonging to that session/transaction will be ended as well.

120.   Which of the following option helps in identifying the expensive statements that are executed very often?
(Only one answer is correct)

(a) System Cache
(b) SQL Plan Cache
(c) SAP HANA Cache
(d) Database Cache

Answer: b

Explanation:

Statement Monitoring

The SQL Plan Cache automatically collects statistics about statement execution. The runtime statistics are aggregated for all executions of the same statement. The statistics collection can be disabled. The Expensive Statements Trace needs to be activated by entering a threshold for the statement runtime.

Afterwards all statements exceeding the specified runtime are logged. Both views are used to analyze long running / expensive SQL statements. While Expensive Statements mainly is used to identify statements, which individually have a long runtime, SQL Plan Cache shows also which statements are expensive because they are executed very often.

121.   Which of the following parameter limits the amount of memory that can be utilized by the database?
    (Only one answer is correct)

    (a) memory_manager_limit
    (b) memory_allocation_limit
    (c) global_manager_limit
    (d) global_allocation_limit

Answer: d

Explanation:

The global_allocation_limit is used to limit the amount of memory which can be used by the database. The value is the maximum allocation limit in MB. A missing entry or a value of 0 results in the system using the default settings (that is, 90% of the physical memory or physical memory minus 1 GB in case of small physical memory). This limit is only displayed on the Configuration tab.
Under the configuration tab, all the parameters can be found and this is the area to maintain parameters for HANA system. In the field Filter, simply type the name of a parameter (or few characters of a parameter); it will display the related parameters with what was typed.

122.   If you have 5 hosts and the limit is set to 5 GB, how much GB can the database use up to?
    (Only one answer is correct)

    (a) 5 GB
    (b) 25 GB
    (c) 10 GB
    (d) 20 GB

Answer: b

Explanation:
Setting the global allocation limit parameter

- Open the Administration Editor by choosing in the navigator toolbar.
- Open the Configuration tab page.
- Open the global.ini parameter group
- Open the memory manager section.
- Choose Change in the context menu for global_allocation_limit.
- Change configuration value dialog box for global_allocation_limit is displayed.

There are two parts to the dialog box which enable you to set this parameter for the entire SYSTEM and for an individual HOST. If it is set for SYSTEM, the value is used for each host. For example, if you have 5 hosts and set the limit to 5 GB, the database can use up to 5GB on each host (25 GB in total). You can additionally set the value for a specific HOST. For that host the specific value is used and the SYSTEM-value is used for all other hosts.

123. **Which of the following isolation level allows seeing the same snapshot of a database? (Only one answer is correct)**

    (a) Transaction level snapshot isolation
    (b) Statement level snapshot isolation
    (c) Concurrency level snapshot isolation
    (d) Redundancy level snapshot isolation

Answer: a

Explanation:

Transaction Isolation Levels

SAP HANA supports both transaction level snapshot isolation and statement level snapshot isolation.
With transaction level snapshot isolation, all statements of a transaction see the same snapshot of the database. This snapshot contains all changes that were committed at the time the transaction started, plus the changes made by the transaction itself. Transaction level snapshot isolation roughly corresponds to SQL isolation level "repeatable read".

124. **Which of the following options exists for adding systems to SAP HANA Studio? (There are two correct answers to the question)**

    (a) Add system
    (b) Add system Link
    (c) Add system Archive link
    (d) Add system using configuration file

Answer: a, c

Explanation:

There are two options available for adding the systems to the SAP HANA studio

- Add System
- Add System Archive Link

The following information is required for the "Add system" option. We need to manually enter the below details for the system to add in HANA
- Host name
- Instance number
- Description (for identification in SAP HANA Studio only)
- Locale
- Database User
- Database Password

The second option allows inserting a link to a centrally-stored archive of SAP HANA systems to allow users who work in the SAP HANA studio to connect efficiently to multiple SAP HANA systems.

125.   **Which of the following are the prerequisites to execute SQL statements in SAP HANA Studio?**
         (Only one answer is correct)

     (a) Systems are added in System View
     (b) Required privileges are there to perform the operation
     (c) You have customized the behavior of SQL statement execution in SQL console
     (d) All of the above

Answer: d

Explanation:

You can execute SQL statements in the SAP HANA studio using the SQL console.

Prerequisites

- You have added the system in the Systems view.
- You have the required privileges to perform the operation.
- You have customized the behavior of SQL statement execution in the SQL console. You can do this in the SAP HANA studio preferences (SAP HANA→Runtime→SQL).

126.   **Which of the following customer specific configuration files are created during installation of SAP HANA database?**
         (Only one answer is correct)

     (a) Sapprofile.ini

(b) Daemon.ini
(c) Nameserver.ini
(d) All of the above

Answer: d

Explanation:

During installation of SAP HANA database, the following customer-specific configuration files are created:

- **sapprofile.ini:** Contains system identification information, such as the system name (SID) or the instance number.
- **daemon.ini:** Contains information about which database services to start.
- **nameserver.ini:** The nameserver.ini file contains global information for each installation.

Multitenant Database Containers

127. **In MDC, which of the following resources will be shared by all the databases?**
     (There are two correct answers to the question)

     (a) Database System software
     (b) Computing resources
     (c) Backups
     (d) Traces and logs

Answer: a, b

Explanation:

All the databases in a multiple container system share the following resources.

- Database Installation System Software
- Same computing resources
- Same System Administration

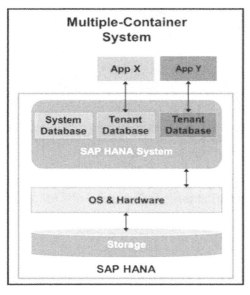

128. **Which of the following statements are correct regarding SAP HANA Multitenant Database containers?**
     (Only one answer is correct)

     (a) Multiple applications can be run on single SAP HANA system
     (b) It is not possible to backup and restore the tenant databases
     (c) Data and users are similar for System DB and Tenant DB
     (d) Integrates well with existing data centre operation procedures

Answer: a, d
Explanation:

SAP HANA Multitenant Database Containers

- Run multiple tenant databases on one SAP HANA system.
- Run and support multiple applications or scenarios on one SAP HANA system in production.
- Strong separation of data and users.
- Backup and restore available by tenant database.
- Resource management by tenant (CPU, Memory).
- Move or copy tenant databases or applications to different hosts or systems.
- Integration with existing data centre operation procedures.

129.   **Which of the following are key trade-offs for a MCOD deployment?**
   (Only one answer is correct)

   (a) Recovery for entire DB
   (b) Negative Impact on Performance
   (c) Additive sizing required
   (d) All of the above

Answer: d

Explanation:

Multiple components on One Database (MCOD)

Multiple applications running on one SAP HANA system are also known as multiple components on One Database (MCOD).

MCOD refers to the scenario where more than one application, scenario or component runs on one SAP HANA system. With this deployment scenario there are few trade-offs for production SAP HANA systems.

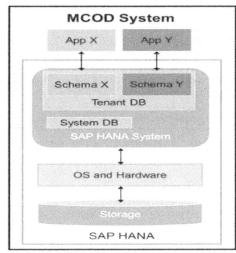

MCOD
- Multiple database schema per database
- Shared SAP HANA database
- Dedicated Application Servers per Application
- Shared hardware, OS, and storage pool
- Key tradeoffs:
  - Contention for resources can negatively impact performance
  - Additive sizing approach required
  - DB recovery available for entire DB (not available per schema)
- Support:
  - Non-production systems
  - Production systems with restrictions (→ see SAP notes)
- SAP notes
  - 1661202 SAP HANA MCOD scenario whitelist
  - 1826100 SAP Business Suite MCOD scenario whitelist
  - 1666670 BW specific considerations

130. **Which of the following resources have a performance impact in MCOS system deployment scenario?**
     (Only one answer is correct)

(a) Memory
(b) CPU
(c) I/O
(d) All of the above

Answer: d

Explanation:

Multiple Components on One System (MCOS)

Multiple SAP HANA systems on one host are also known as multiple components on one system. SAP does support running multiple instances in single production SAP HANA host. With this deployment you need a significant attention to administrative tasks and performance management.
Running multiple systems on single host will have an impact on performance and will have competition among the computing resources such Memory, CPU, I/O and so on.

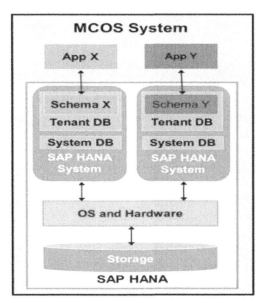

131.   Which of the following would be the benefit of using Virtualization?
       (There are two correct answers to the question)

(a) Dedicated resources
(b) Flexibility
(c) Easily Scalable
(d) Very Less Expensive

Answer: a, b

Explanation:

SAP HANA Supports virtualization supervisors such as

•   VMware vSphere 5.1 or newer
•   Hitachi LPAR
•   Huawei Fusion Sphere
•   IBM Power VM or other for non-production environments

SAP HANA with virtualization refers to the scenario where one or more SAP HANA database SIDs is deployed on one or more virtual machines running on SAP HANA server hardware. One benefit of using virtualization is that you can assign dedicated CPU and memory resources to specific databases and increase the flexibility of hardware usage.

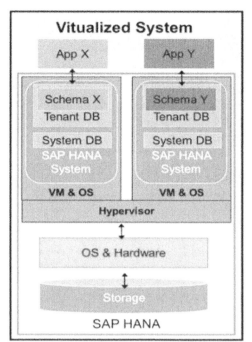

Virtualization
- One database schema per database
- Separate SAP HANA databases per SAP system
- Separate virtual machine and OS
- Shared hardware and storage
- Details about the supported scenarios:
  - SAP Note 1788665 – SAP HANA Support for virtualized / partitioned (multi-tenant) environments

132. **Which of the following scenarios are suitable for technical co-deployment? (Only one answer is correct)**

   (a) Single Node
   (b) Production Systems
   (c) Virtualization
   (d) All of the above

Answer: d

Explanation:
Technical co deployment is an alternative that can be used to combine with several applications. This is available for Supplier Relationship Management (SRM) and Supply Chain Management (SCM). It is provided as an SAP ERP add on and can be used productively.

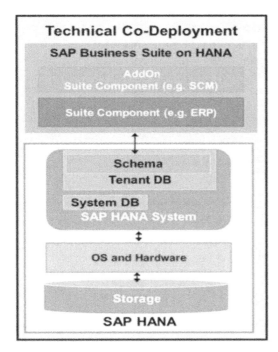

133.   Which of the following a tenant database will have?
(Only one answer is correct)

(a) Traces
(b) Logs
(c) Persistence
(d) All of the above

Answer: d

Explanation:

All the databases in multi container systems share the same database system software, the same computing resources, and the same system administration. They have the following features

- Tenant databases are identified by name or port
- Additive sizing for all tenant databases
- Strong isolation features, so that each tenant database has the following
    - ✓ Database Administration and end users
    - ✓ Database Catalog
    - ✓ Traces
    - ✓ Logs
    - ✓ Persistence
    - ✓ Backups
- Tenant memory sizing and CPU consumption can be configured independently.

134.   Which of the following statements are true regarding System DB?

(There are two correct answers to the question)

(a) Scale out of System DB is possible
(b) Scale out of System DB is not possible
(c) System DB can show monitoring data of Tenant DB
(d) System DB is database with full SQL support

Answer: b, c

Explanation:

System Database is created during installation of a multiple container system or during the conversion of database from a single container system to multiple container system. System Database has the following features

- System DB is not a database with full SQL support.
- It cannot be distributed with multiple hosts, i.e., scale out is not possible
- You must create a tenant database to have a full featured SAP HANA database is multiple container system.
- System databases can show monitoring data from tenant databases.

135. **Which of the following are the properties of a system with a high isolation level?**
     (Only one answer is correct)

(a) Process for tenant DB runs under its own users.
(b) Database specific data on the file system is protected using OS file and directory permissions
(c) OS access is restricted to users with the correct permissions
(d) All of the above

Answer: d

Explanation:

The database isolation specifies the isolation of the tenant databases on the operating system level for multitenant database container SAP HANA systems. By default, all the process in multi container system runs under the <sid>adm OS user.

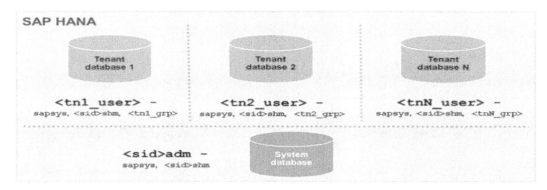

The properties of a system with the high isolation are as follows:

- Individual tenant database process runs under its dedicated OS users belonging to dedicated OS groups.
- Database specific data on the file system is protected by OS file and directory permissions. <sid>adm user will not have access to tenant database volumes or backups but it can access tenant specific trace and configuration files.
- Tenant administrator with OS access cannot access other tenant or System databases using the OS commands.
- Operations that require OS access is restricted to users with correct permission this add another layer of security for tenant databases.

136. **Which of the following app indicates the overall system health of a Database?**
   (Only one answer is correct)

   (a) Overall Tenant statuses
   (b) Top tenant databases with Alerts
   (c) System status
   (d) System Monitoring and Administration

Answer: a

Explanation:

Overall Tenant Statuses:
This indicates the overall system health. It provides access to Manage Database App where we can monitor the status and resource usage of Individual databases and perform other administrative tasks.

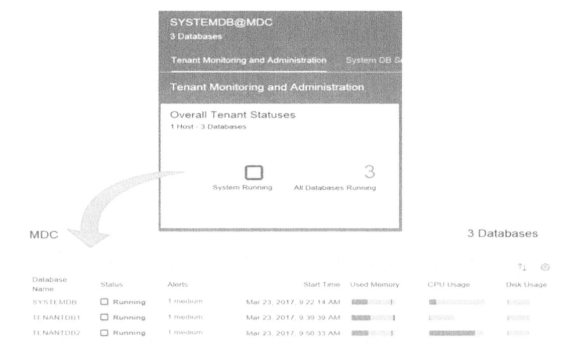

137. **Which of the following are the different ways of creating and configuring a tenant database?**
    (There are two correct answers to the question)

(a) Manage Database App
(b) SQL Command
(c) Through a Background job
(d) Using a script

Answer: a, b

Explanation:

During the installation of HANA database, only System Database will be created initially. We can create and configure the tenant database using Manage Database App in SAP HANA cockpit or using the SQL command CREATE DATABASE. This new tenant database is created and started and appears in Overall Tenant Status App.

SQL Command:

CREATE DATABASE <DBNAME> SYSTEM USER PASSWORD <PWD>

SAP HANA Cockpit:

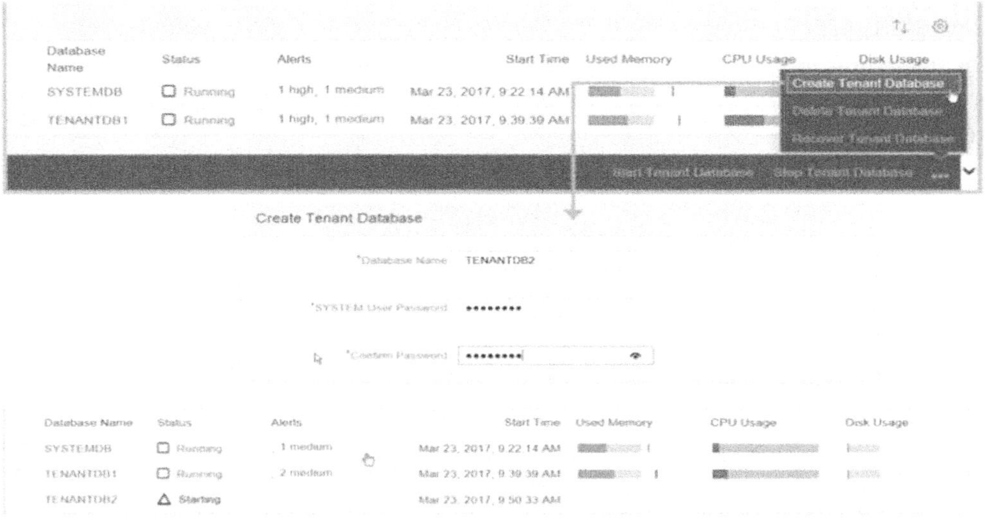

138.   **Which of the following is the maximum number of tenant databases that can be created per instance?**
(Only one answer is correct)

(a) 20
(b) 10
(c) 30
(d) 40

Answer: a

Explanation:

- Every tenant database in a multi container system has dedicated ports for SQL, HTTP based communication and internal communication.
- The default port number range for tenant database is 3<instance>40 – 3<instance>99.
- This means the maximum number of instances that can be created per instance are 20. However, this can be increased by reserving the port numbers for further instances.
- You can change the parameter [multidb] reserved_instance_numbers property in the global.ini file. The default value for this property is 0 and if you change it to 1, port number for further one instance is available.

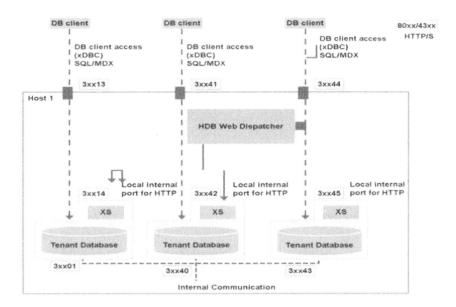

139. Which of the following additional layer facilitates for configuring the system properties for individual databases?
    (Only one answer is correct)

    (a) Host
    (b) Database
    (c) Service
    (d) System

Answer: b

Explanation:

The configuration files (*.ini) of the SAP HANA system contain properties for the whole system as well individual tenant database, hosts and services.

In multiple container systems, configuration files have an additional layer database which facilitates in configuring the properties for the individual tenant databases as well. Properties configured at system level will apply for all the databases whereas properties configured at database level will apply only to a specific database.

For properties that are configured at system, host and database level, the value configured at database level takes precedence.

140. Which of the following properties are particularly useful for influencing the resource consumption of tenant databases?
    (There are two correct answers to the questions)

    (a) Memory
    (b) CPU

(c) Network
(d) Disk Throughput

Answer: a, b

Explanation:

For individual tenant databases, we can manage and control the memory and CPU usage by configuring the limits in the system properties files. The following properties particularly useful for influencing the resource consumption of tenant databases:

Memory: This limits the maximum amount of memory that can be allocated to all the processes of a given tenant database.
CPU: This limits the number of concurrently running threads used by the SAP HANA job executor.

141. **Which of the following are the properties of multitenant database container backup and recovery?**
     (Only one answer is correct)

    (a) Recovery is always initiated by the System Database
    (b) Tenant Database will have their own backup Catalog
    (c) Snapshots are currently not supported for tenant databases
    (d) All of the above

Answer: d

Explanation:

The following are the specific properties of multitenant database container backup and recovery:

- The system database plays a crucial role and it can initiate backups for system database and tenant databases. And recoveries are always performed by System Database.
- Tenant databases also can carry out their own backups unless it is prohibited in the system configuration.
- System database and tenant databases have their own backup Catalog.
- Backup location in the file system is specified system wide. Backups of tenant databases are always created in subdirectories of this location.
- Snapshots are currently not supported for multitenant database containers

142. **Which of the following statements are correct regarding tenant database recovery?**
     (There are two correct answers to the question)

    (a) Tenant database can be recovered only from System database
    (b) Tenant database recovery can be initiated by tenant database itself
    (c) System DB and all other tenant DBs will be offline during recovery
    (d) System DB and other tenant DBs are not affected during recovery

Answer: a, d

Explanation:

Recovering a tenant Database: To recover the tenant database, proceed as follows

- Initiate the tenant database recovery from the system database.
- The system database and other tenant databases are not affected.
- Select the tenant database you want to recover
- Specify the recovery type and required setting for the recovery and start the recovery.

Note: During the tenant database recovery, system database and all other tenant databases remains online. The system does not support the tenant database copy using backup and recovery with the third party tools. A backup of tenant database can be recovered to the different SAP HANA multitenant database container using file system based backups.

Made in the USA
Las Vegas, NV
14 April 2021